CRITICAL

ANTONY AND

CLEOPATRA

William Shakespeare

Editors:
Linda Cookson
Bryan Loughrey

LONGMAN
LITERATURE
GUIDES

Longman Literature Guides

Editors: Linda Cookson and Bryan Loughrey

Titles in the series:

CONTENTS

PREFACE

Like all professional groups, literary critics have developed their own specialised language. This is not necessarily a bad thing. Sometimes complex concepts can only be described in a terminology far removed from everyday speech. Academic jargon, however, creates an unnecessary barrier between the critic and the intelligent but less practised reader.

This danger is particularly acute where scholarly books and articles are re-packaged for a student audience. Critical anthologies, for example, often contain extracts from longer studies originally written for specialists. Deprived of their original context, these passages can puzzle and at times mislead. The essays in this volume, however, are all specially commissioned, self-contained works, written with the needs of students firmly in mind.

This is not to say that the contributors — all experienced critics and teachers — have in any way attempted to simplify the complexity of the issues with which they deal. On the contrary, they explore the central problems of the text from a variety of critical perspectives, reaching conclusions which are challenging and at times mutually contradictory.

They try, however, to present their arguments in direct, accessible language and to work within the limitations of scope and length which students inevitably face. For this reason, essays are generally rather briefer than is the practice; they address quite specific topics; and, in line with examination requirements, they incorporate precise textual detail into the body of the discussion.

They offer, therefore, working examples of the kind of essay-writing skills which students themselves are expected to develop. Their diversity, however, should act as a reminder that in the field of literary studies there is no such thing as a 'model' answer. Good essays are the outcome of a creative engagement with literature, of sensitive, attentive reading and careful thought. We hope that those contained in this volume will encourage students to return to the most important starting point of all, the text itself, with renewed excitement and the determination to explore more fully their own critical responses.

How to use this volume

Obviously enough, you should start by reading the text in question. The one assumption that all the contributors make is that you are already familiar with this. It would be helpful, of course, to have read further — perhaps other works by the same author or by influential contemporaries. But we don't assume that you have yet had the opportunity to do this and any references to historical background or to other works of literature are explained.

You should, perhaps, have a few things to hand. It is always a good idea to keep a copy of the text nearby when reading critical studies. You will almost certainly want to consult it when checking the context of quotations or pausing to consider the validity of the critic's interpretation. You should also try to have access to a good dictionary, and ideally a copy of a dictionary of literary terms as well. The contributors have tried to avoid jargon and to express themselves clearly and directly. But inevitably there will be occasional words or phrases with which you are unfamiliar. Finally, we would encourage you to make notes, summarising not just the argument of each essay but also your own responses to what you have read. So keep a pencil and notebook at the ready.

Suitably equipped, the best thing to do is simply begin with whichever topic most interests you. We have deliberately organised each volume so that the essays may be read in any order. One consequence of this is that, for the sake of clarity and self-containment, there is occasionally a degree of overlap between essays. But at least you are not forced to follow one — fairly arbitrary — reading sequence.

Each essay is followed by brief 'Afterthoughts', designed to highlight points of critical interest. But remember, these are only there to remind you that it is *your* responsibility to question what you read. The essays printed here are not a series of 'model' answers to be slavishly imitated and in no way should they be regarded as anything other than a guide or stimulus for your own thinking. We hope for a critically involved response: 'That was interesting. But if *I* were tackling the topic . . .!'

Read the essays in this spirit and you'll pick up many of the skills of critical composition in the process. We have, however, tried to provide more explicit advice in 'A practical guide to essay writing'. You may find this helpful, but do not imagine it offers any magic formulas. The quality of your essays ultimately depends on the quality of your engagement with literary texts. We hope this volume spurs you on to read these with greater understanding and to explore your responses in greater depth.

A note on the text

All references are to the New Penguin Shakespeare edition of Antony and Cleopatra, ed. Emrys Jones.

Kate Flint

Kate Flint is Fellow and Tutor in
English Literature at Mansfield College,
Oxford. She is the author of numerous
critical works.

ESSAY

Significant otherness: sex, silence and Cleopatra

Antony and Cleopatra is a play about sex, and about politics. All other issues — honour, leadership, loyalty, personal integrity — are inseparable from these two intimately related elements. But neither sexuality nor political beliefs are seen in the same way during all periods, or by all people, as becomes immediately clear when we look at the stage history of Shakespeare's play. To look at how these crucial areas have been constructed at various times in the past therefore raises two major questions. First, how may we, today, see the play in relation to sexual and international politics now? And second, and more essentially, what is it about the play which has made it such a popular springboard for the dramatisation of various current preoccupations and prejudices?

For both directors and critics, the source of the play's sexuality has invariably been Cleopatra herself. Her power to allure and to command is legendary. And when she is brought into the theatre, the dynamics and effects of her power made visible, her portrayal can be seen to dramatise the prevailing gender assumptions and sexual stereotyping of a period. In the nineteenth century in particular, she was presented as a figure who threatened the concept of decorous womanhood. Her seductiveness was seen as dangerous: the power of the 'enchanting queen' was presented as being gained not through recognisable forms of political astuteness, but through her very difference from men, whose public politics she manipulated through her private sexual games. Indeed, the lines in which she describes to Mardian how:

> . . . I drunk him [Antony] to his bed;
> Then put my tires and mantles on him, whilst
> I wore his sword Philippan

(II.5.21–23)

or the reference to her hopping forty paces in the public street, were, like the bawdy conversation which Cleopatra holds with her women about where they would like to find extra inches on their men's anatomy, considered far too shocking actually to be spoken on the Victorian stage. Thus productions played up what contemporary critics called her 'histrionic resources'; her capacity to change mood quickly; and what one writer termed the 'lurking devil' in her, the 'Oriental cruelty' which showed itself as much in gratuitous violence upon the messenger as in the moment when she callously abandons Antony during the sea-battle. She was what Victorian men officially most distrusted and condemned in women: no angel in the house, full of maternal concern, but a woman with an energetic enjoyment of sexuality, taking the lead in erotic play: a woman with an irresponsible playfulness, an unsettling changeability, and the capacity to divert a man from both profession and wife. Antony, as the play opens, is no longer an admirable captain, but 'The triple pillar of the world transformed/ Into a strumpet's fool' (I.1.12–13), to quote Philo's sneering judgement. Yet, just as paintings in mid-nineteenth-century art exhibitions of Eastern harems, baths and slave markets, full of figures of semi-clothed Oriental women, provided an excuse for a socially acceptable form of mild pornography, so stage representations of Cleopatra seem to have offered a similar opportunity for a vicarious enjoyment of female sexuality. By the end of the century, she was even being played by someone who could legitimately be called a sex-symbol in her own right: the mistress of the Prince of Wales, Lillie Langtry. Langtry herself was in no doubt as to where the emphasis should lie in her performance — 'We all know that Cleopatra was a great coquette and subjugator of men', and as she goes on to relate in her autobiography, was somewhat aggrieved to have found that the play didn't aid her image as much as she'd hoped, discovering that the love scenes were 'very short, and contain a great deal of bickering'. The sense of Cleopatra being linked to sexual spectacle was emphasised by the Victorian and Edwardian tendency to turn Shakespeare into near-circus. So she appeared on stage accompanied by processions, specially commissioned ballets and realistic battles at sea; she was rowed across stage in 'the barge she sat on', Enobarbus's description of how the Egyptian's seductive power overawed Antony thus being robbed of its mystery through being given material form.

Yet when, as in some more recent twentieth-century productions, Cleopatra has been presented as a more conventionally shrewd political animal, critics have castigated her for not being different enough from men; not conforming closely enough to current ideals of sexual attractiveness. A different type of powerfulness poses a different type of threat. Thus, for example, Glenda Jackson, playing Cleopatra with a gutsy directness in 1978 for the RSC, was variously criticised by reviewers for 'her Cub-mistress heartiness and no-nonsense cropped hair', for having 'unpromising features', for creating the impression that she was about to 'thwack her thighs and invite us all to a jolly game of hockey'. As one (male) critic wrote, these physical disadvantages 'seriously dent Cleopatra's reputation as a classical sex symbol'. Yet, to quote Glenda Jackson herself, if one attempts to play the part mainly on the level of Cleopatra's attractiveness, 'then you are on a hiding to nothing. You always suffer anyway from measuring up to what is considered to be attractive and desirable in a woman'. The tendency has been, perhaps, to underestimate the extent of Cleopatra's attractiveness to Antony, and to Shakespeare's own audience, as the play presents it. For her power and attraction lie not just in her controlled physical sexuality and in her calculatedly capricious temperament, but in the public position she holds, in her power to despatch, reward, punish and command. This may well have been apparent to those who had been accustomed to Queen

Elizabeth's rule; it is certainly obvious to anyone who observes the press treatment of a forceful woman prime minister in our own time. Scarus is contemptuous of Antony's battle tactics, and — by implication — of Cleopatra's:

> ...like a doting mallard,
> Leaving the fight in height, flies after her.
> I never saw an action of such shame.
> Experience, manhood, honour, ne'er before
> Did violate so itself.
>
> (III.10.19–23)

But it is *Antony* whom the action shows most to be at fault, unable to keep the separate demands made by separate spheres of his life apart: Scarus merely voices a common male fear of woman's capacity to lead man astray, and fails to give weight to the pragmatic way in which the Egyptian ruler looks after her country's own interests.

This habit of seeing Cleopatra through men's eyes, defined through her attractiveness towards them and her difference, her otherness from them, has been compounded and complicated in its effects by her equation with the Orient. The Orient, according to Edward Said in *Orientalism*, has long been one of Europe's 'deepest and most recurrent images of the Other'. Stage design, especially in the latter half of the nineteenth century, the heyday of English colonialist policies, readily lent itself to a type of cultural imperialism which borrowed and adapted visual images of the Orient without ever needing to pause and consider its complexity. Alexandrian splendour was invariably stressed to the exclusion of the overtly political scenes set in Rome, and was represented with reference to fashions in interior decoration and the reiterated stereotypes of Egyptian tourism: sphinxes and hieroglyphics.

In the twentieth century, however, the Roman scenes were largely reinstated, and different international concerns gave directors different political reference points. Following the 1939–45 war, the image of the significant gap was no longer that between Orient and West, but between democracy and authoritarianism. This could be reinterpreted in terms of the perceived distance between the amount of humanity shown in the personal, albeit obviously fallible, relationship between

Antony and Cleopatra, and the world of cold, militaristic Rome, where things are done, calculatingly, 'by the rule'. Such an interpretation ignores, of course, the calculating politics of which Cleopatra, in particular, is capable — in deciding, for example, when the opportune moment to withdraw her ships or withhold a proportion of her jewels may be. It ignores, too, the fact that the most decadent of all scenes, the drunken revelry aboard Pompey's galley, takes place in Rome: West and East are not such separate worlds, by any means, as many commentators on this play have made them out to be. Corruption, efficiency, courage and despotism may be found in either: it is worth speculating what effect current political changes in Eastern Europe may bring to future stage interpretations of Shakespeare's play.

So what is it about the presentation of Cleopatra, and of her Oriental setting, which has rendered her so vulnerable to changing points of view? For Shakespeare's text is not inherently sexist or racist, despite making dramatic capital of the fact that differences exist between men and women, and between cultures. But it does place us in a position where we, whether female or male, are looking on at Cleopatra. Moreover, we always observe and judge her acting within a sphere which is to some degree public. She speaks no soliloquies: we never see her in private, from within. Her speeches are always tuned to others' ears. She recognises from the start that it is unwise to remain for long immersed in intimate concerns, however pleasant: she challenges Antony's grandiose protestations:

> Let Rome in Tiber melt, and the wide arch
> Of the ranged empire fall! Here is my space

(I.1.33–34)

by bidding him hear the messengers from Rome. Though this may be one more form of flirtation, testing the firmness of his interest in her, it can also be understood as a signal of her continuous pragmatic alertness. The importance of her attitude towards the messengers lies ultimately in the way in which it resists confident explanation. Only occasionally do we see her lose control, most notably, and tellingly, with the messenger from Rome whom she fears brings her bad news about Antony. But after striking him, pulling him around by the hair, and verbally abusing him, she recalls this unfortunate man and demonstrates, through her dialogue, her capacity to use language as a far more effective means of transformative power than physical cruelty: the fact that Octavia is shorter than she, and 'low-voiced', is instantly transmuted into the belittling, but memorable 'Dull of tongue, and dwarfish' (III.3.16).

Whilst hardly presenting her in a likeable light, these scenes have a further dramatic point beyond showing Cleopatra's volatility. They show the difficulty for someone who is perpetually in the public gaze of finding a means through which they can safely express emotions and anxieties. Even when Cleopatra is with close women companions, those companions persist in making her aware of her status, and difference from them. As she swoons at Antony's death, Charmian and Iras call out to her:

> CHARMIAN   O, quietness, lady!
> IRAS   She's dead too, our sovereign.
> CHARMIAN   Lady!
> IRAS   Madam!
> CHARMIAN   O madam, madam, madam!
> IRAS   Royal Egypt! Empress!

> (IV.15.68–71)

Even though Cleopatra, reviving, begs 'No more', claiming that she is:

> . . . e'en a woman, and commanded
> By such poor passion as the maid that milks
> And does the meanest chares

> (IV.13.72–74)

the vocabulary of sceptre and jewel through which she immediately emphasises her loss shows the gap, in fact, between the mental worlds in which courtiers and queen separately move. Although earlier in the play we've seen her joking with them, their reactions, however touchingly loyal, at this point in the play serve to dramatise how hard it is for one in Cleopatra's position to have, even if she wants it, a friendship among equals. This, of course, was one of the attractions of Antony for her: if not sexually equivalent, they could, at least, recognise a mutuality when it came to other forms of power relations.

Immediately after her revival into consciousness, we are

reminded of the attention Cleopatra habitually pays to self-presentation, to theatrical impact. Early in the play she warns, in relation to Antony's marriage to Fulvia, that 'I'll seem the fool I am not' (I.1.42) in order to goad him on the subject. According to Enobarbus, her initial appearance before his master at Cydnus was a *tour-de-force* of pageantry used, as Queen Elizabeth had used it, both to show off material wealth and to symbolise almost magical power. In private, as we have seen, she plays role-reversal games of dress in putting on Antony's 'sword Philippan'. But her most conspicuous act of staging takes place in the final scenes of the play. After she has despatched Antony's body for burial, she makes a barely concealed reference to suicide, which will be performed like a display for death's benefit:

> . . . what's brave, what's noble,
> Let's do't after the high Roman fashion,
> And make death proud to take us.

(IV.15.85–87)

Following Antony's bungled attempt at falling on his sword, moreover, this seems like one final attempt to outdo even her favourite partner in Roman efficiency. As we see in the last scene, Cleopatra costumes herself to meet death in robe and crown, commanding her women to act like stage managers:

> Show me, my women, like a queen; go fetch
> My best attires. I am again for Cydnus,
> To meet Mark Antony.

(V.2.227–229)

Critical

Cleopatra's desire to die nobly is not merely, however, a wish to rejoin her lover in the after-life, or an enactment of the world's emptiness now that he is gone. It is a means of preserving her identity, and of being in command of the terms on which others observe her. She is apprehensive about being paraded, at second hand, in Rome, the subject of theatrical spectacle controlled and performed by others. To conquer Cleopatra in political terms brings with it, she perceives, the ability, if not the right, to interpret and re-present her according to the clichés, even, of her own setting. Moreover, such tawdry pageantry is expressed by her in terms which reveal not just her own sense of class superiority, but her physical revulsion that others may come too close to her, even to an image of her, without her choosing. She addresses Iras:

> Mechanic slaves
> With greasy aprons, rules, and hammers shall
> Uplift us to the view. In their thick breaths,
> Rank of gross diet, shall we be enclouded,
> And forced to drink their vapour.
>   . . . Saucy lictors
> Will catch at us like strumpets, and scald rhymers
> Ballad us out o'tune. The quick comedians
> Extemporally will stage us, and present
> Our Alexandrian revels. Antony
> Shall be brought drunken forth, and I shall see
> Some squeaking Cleopatra boy my greatness
> I'th'posture of a whore.

(V.2.209–221)

It is Cleopatra, at the last, who draws attention to the dangers inherent in dramatising her role according to stereotypes, particularly the sexual stereotypes which are temptingly, for some, suggested by the broad outlines of her story. Such staging will belittle the complexities of the power which she has wielded, and the degree to which she is determined to maintain her integrity in the face of the conflicting pressures of private and public worlds. But since Shakespeare allows no consistent vision of what the private, solitary Cleopatra's consciousness might consist of, she will always remain resistant to interpretation, as women more generally have resisted many attempts by men to describe and confine them; as the Orient has been the consistent victim of many oversimplifying Western clichés. Cleopatra's ultimate power lies in her silence, as the play presents it, in never revealing for more than a few moments what her private thoughts may be.

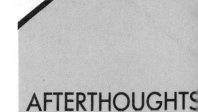
1

Do you agree that Cleopatra 'looks after her country's own interests' (page 12)?

2

Do you agree with Flint that we never see Cleopatra 'in private, from within' (page 13)?

3

What arguments does Flint put forward in this essay to show the 'dangers' of dramatising Cleopatra's role 'according to stereotypes' (page 16)?

4

The role of Cleopatra would have been played on the Jacobean stage by a boy actor. Does this fact in any way qualify Flint's argument?

Alan Gardiner

Alan Gardiner is Lecturer in English Language and Literature at Redbridge Technical College, and is the author of numerous critical studies.

ESSAY

Leadership in *Antony and Cleopatra*

In Shakespeare's plays the study of politics is generally the study of the individual character rather than of collective human behaviour. The plays do not propound political theories but give us a compelling sense of the human realities of politics. Matters of great historical moment are viewed in terms of the personalities involved — their longings and their insecurities, their relationships with each other, their reactions to the possession of political power (or to the loss of it). Shakespeare's interest is in the forces that drive people to seek power, the ways in which power changes hands and the nature of the psychological burden that those in positions of authority must carry. He is especially interested in exposing the human frailty and vulnerability of those who wield great political power. We see this interest when Macbeth feels his heart knock against his ribs after the witches have prophesied that he will become king, when Richard III cries before the Battle of Bosworth 'O Ratcliffe, I fear, I fear!' and when Richard II tells his followers:

> I live with bread, like you; feel want,
> Taste grief, need friends. Subjected thus,
> How can you say to me, I am a king?

(III.2.175)

Shakespeare's presentation of the triumvirs of the Roman Empire in *Antony and Cleopatra* is consistent with this approach: the triple pillars of the world can be touchy, ill-tempered and hysterical, and are seen shedding tears and getting drunk. It is also the case that the analysis of Roman politics focuses on individuals at or near the centre of power: on Antony, Caesar and Lepidus, and on Pompey, who briefly threatens the rule of the triumvirs. The general populace is referred to only briefly, though these references are telling, creating the impression of a shifting, unstable society:

> This common body,
> Like to a vagabond flag upon the stream,
> Goes to and back, lackeying the varying tide,
> To rot itself with motion.
>
> (I.4.44–47)

This instability is mirrored in the attitudes and actions of Rome's political leaders, with their factional in-fighting and fragile pacts and allegiances.

In such a society Lepidus is clearly ill-equipped to succeed. This is evident from his first appearance in the play, when he is seen in conversation with Caesar (I.4). Caesar dominates the dialogue and when the two messengers arrive with news of Pompey's rebellion they address themselves to him, ignoring Lepidus's presence entirely. At the close of the scene Lepidus has to ask Caesar to notify him of any further developments. However, although the scene underlines his political ineffectiveness, we also glimpse in Lepidus an appealing sensitivity and generosity of nature. His defence of Antony implies a recognition that what Caesar perceives as Antony's 'faults' are at the same time colourful and attractive qualities:

> His faults, in him, seem as the spots of heaven,
> More fiery by night's blackness . . .
>
> (I.4.12–13)

It is characteristic of Lepidus that he should seek to reduce Caesar's hostility towards Antony; in his other appearances in the play he is consistently the voice of conciliation. Before Antony's meeting with Caesar he urges Enobarbus 'to entreat your captain/ To soft and gentle speech' and, alluding to the threat from Pompey, observes that it is 'not a time/ For private stomaching' (II.2.2–3, 8–9). His attitude seems more sensible than Enobarbus's belligerent hope that 'If Caesar move him,/ Let Antony look over Caesar's head/ And speak as loud as Mars' (II.2.4–6). But although Lepidus shows some wisdom and insight, his lack of personal authority and assertiveness makes him a political lightweight. He says little during Antony's confrontation with Caesar and similarly makes a minimal contribution to the talks with Pompey (II.6). His shortcomings are given the most damning emphasis in the scene on board Pompey's galley (II.7). The servants speak contemptuously of his drunkenness, and comment on his inadequacy as a triumvir:

> To be called into a huge sphere, and not to be seen to move in't, are the holes where eyes should be, which pitifully disaster the cheeks.

> (II.7.14–16)

He is too drunk to realise that he is the butt of a joke when Antony describes to him the Egyptian crocodile, which is 'shaped, sir, like itself' and 'as broad as it hath breadth' (II.7.42–43). His final indignity is to be carried off by an attendant. A few scenes later Lepidus is again the object of derision, as Enobarbus and Agrippa mock his devotion to Antony and Caesar, which is seen as of an unmanly extravagance:

> But he loves Caesar best, yet he loves Antony —
> Hoo! Hearts, tongues, figures, scribes, bards, poets cannot
> Think, speak, cast, write, sing, number — hoo! —
> His love to Antony. But as for Caesar,
> Kneel down, kneel down, and wonder.

> (III.2.15–19)

The contempt in which Lepidus is held may arouse some sympathy for him in the audience, but it is also clear that he is too feeble to survive for long the treacherous machinations of Roman politics. Caesar, having made use of him in the wars ''gainst Pompey' (III.5.6–7), removes him from the triumvirate with no apparent difficulty and with little attempt at justification — the allegation that Lepidus had 'grown too cruel' (III.6.32) is manifestly unconvincing.

Antony is capable of commanding the kind of respect that

Lepidus lacks, though it is significant that he is admired for his skill in the military rather than the political sphere. Philo evokes a figure of god-like power and strength, whose eyes 'Have glowed like plated Mars' and whose exertions in battle have 'burst/ The buckles on his breast' (I.1.4, 7–8); Caesar recalls Antony's past endurance of extreme hardship, hardship that 'Was borne so like a soldier' (I.4.70); Pompey fears Antony's return from Egypt because, in comparison with the other triumvirs, 'His soldiership/ Is twice the other twain' (II.1.34–35). In striking contrast to Caesar, Antony's authority as a leader also derives from attractive personal qualities, from the warmth and magnanimity of his nature. This aspect of his character is well described in Plutarch:

> Furthermore, things that seeme intollerable in other men, as to boast commonly, to jeast with one or other, to drinke like a good fellow with everybody, to sit with the souldiers when they dine, and to eate and drinke with them souldierlike: it is incredible what wonderfull love it wanne him amongest them. And furthermore, being given to love: that made him the more desired, and by that meanes he brought many to love him ... But besides all this, that which most procured his rising and advauncement, was his liberalitie, who gave all to the souldiers, and kept nothing for him selfe: and when he was grown to great credit, then was his authoritie and power also very great.
>
> (cited in *Antony and Cleopatra*, Arden edition, London, 1989, Appendix V, p. 241)

In the play itself there is ample evidence of Antony's openness and generosity. In the first scene, he suggests to Cleopatra that they 'wander through the streets and note/ The qualities of people' (I.1.53–54) and Caesar later speaks disapprovingly of his readiness to drink with slaves. After the naval defeat at Actium, he offers his attendants a ship laden with gold and urges them to make their peace with Caesar. In a similar gesture, Antony sends Enobarbus's treasure on to him after his desertion. We see also the devotion that this kind of behaviour can inspire when Enobarbus dies of a broken heart and when Eros decides to take his own life rather than that of his master.

However, it is perhaps a failing in Antony as a leader that the affection he shows his followers is not accompanied by much thought as to its likely effects. When he asks Eros to take his life, Antony is guilty of an insensitivity to his feelings of loyalty and devotion, and Eros's reaction is as the audience might have predicted. The response of Antony's attendants to his emotional speech after Actium ('Fly? not we') is similarly unsurprising, as is Enobarbus's despair when Antony despatches his treasure together with 'gentle adieus, and greetings'. Howard Jacobson has a point when he remarks that 'Antony's generosity is something it might be better not to be on the receiving end of'.[1]

If we should be careful not to view with unqualified approval Antony's liberality, we should also not exaggerate his followers' fidelity. The battle at Actium is scarcely over before Canidius decides to surrender his legions to Caesar, following the example of six kings who 'Show me the way of yielding' (III.10.34). A few scenes later Caesar can claim:

> Within our files there are,
> Of those that served Mark Antony but late,
> Enough to fetch him in.

> (IV.1.12–14)

After Antony's bungled attempt at suicide the guards abandon him, ignoring his pleas that they finish what he has begun. Decretas lingers only to take Antony's sword, in the hope that 'This sword but shown to Caesar, with his tidings,/ Shall enter me with him' (II.14.112–113).

Such actions illustrate the self-interest which pervades the Roman Empire as it is presented in the play, but they also indicate the extent to which Antony's conduct of the war against Caesar undermines the high esteem in which he is held by his men. The campaign begins with the calamitous decision to accept Caesar's challenge to fight at sea. Antony's followers remind him that his men are better equipped for a land battle, that they are unaccustomed to naval warfare and that Antony's own 'renownèd knowledge' as a military leader is best employed on land (III.7.45). Antony ignores their advice, his decision based not on strategy but on bravado — he will fight Caesar at

---

[1] *Shakespeare's Magnanimity* (London, 1978).

sea because 'he dares us to't' (III.7.29). The ensuing engagement ends not only in inevitable defeat but in disgrace, with Antony fleeing the battle in pursuit of Cleopatra. The verdict of his men is accurate and unsparing:

> The great cantle of the world is lost
> With very ignorance. We have kissed away
> Kingdoms and provinces.
>
> (III.10.6–8)

> I never saw an action of such shame
> Experience, manhood, honour, ne'er before
> Did violate so itself.
>
> (III.10.21–23)

The absurd challenge to Caesar to settle the war by personal combat is mocked by Enobarbus and provokes similar derision in Caesar himself. The demeaning loss of self-control Antony demonstrates in ordering Thidias to be whipped (III.13) suggests a desperate attempt to regain the authority he has lost, emphasising the truthfulness of his own acknowledgement that 'Authority melts from me' (III.13.90) and of his earlier admission 'I have lost command' (III.11.23).

The weaknesses Antony displays during the war with Caesar — impetuousness, lack of judgement and of self-discipline — are less apparent in the earlier political scenes in Rome. There is a tetchiness in his initial exchanges with Caesar (II.2), but the manner of his subsequent response to the accusations against him is both confident and diplomatic, conceding that there is some justification in what Caesar says but refusing to be intimidated. His agreement to the marriage with Octavia, however, shows a characteristic lack of forethought. It extricates him from his immediate difficulties but he does not consider the political repercussions of the marriage failing — as fail it must. Enobarbus — perhaps Caesar too — knows the marriage will not last, and Antony himself, just one scene after the marriage has been agreed, declares 'I will to Egypt...I'th'East my pleasure lies' (II.3.39–41). As soon as Antony leaves Rome he begins to be outmanoeuvred by Caesar, who makes war on Pompey and disposes of Lepidus, clearing the way for the elimination of Antony. While Caesar acts with speed, determination and efficiency,

Antony's response to these events when he learns of them in Athens is marked by a conspicuous absence of all these qualities: we hear that he is 'walking in the garden', ranting against the officer who murdered Pompey (III.5.16). His management of the war that follows is, as has been seen, disastrous.

Antony loses in the struggle between the triumvirs because Caesar's character is ideally suited to the world of Roman politics while his is not — Antony is open and spontaneous where Caesar is calculating and duplicitous, without political ambition where Caesar is determined to rule the empire alone, and confused and irresolute where Caesar has always a clear vision of his ultimate objectives. Caesar is dedicated to the achievement of his political ends and, as we see from his consent to Octavia's marriage to Antony, personal relationships are secondary to this aim. He subsequently uses the marriage's failure as partial justification for the war against Antony. Enobarbus's prediction that the marriage would eventually cause conflict between Antony and Caesar strengthens our suspicion that Caesar himself had anticipated this. Certainly in Plutarch, Caesar is keen to exploit difficulties in the marriage: when Octavia wishes to leave Rome to join Antony:

> her brother Octavius Caesar was willing unto it, not for his respect at all (as most authors doe report) as for that he might have an honest culler (= colour) to make warre with Antonius if he did misuse her, and not esteeme of her as she ought to be.
>
> (cited in *Antony and Cleopatra*, Arden edition, London, 1989, Appendix V, p. 256)

During the war itself, Caesar commands his forces with confidence and skill. In its early stages Canidius observes that 'This speed of Caesar's/ Carries beyond belief' (III.7.74–75) and the series of short scenes that follows gives a vivid impression of his irresistible advance. The war scenes also give an insight into Caesar's style of leadership, a style very different from Antony's. There is none of the camaraderie evident in Antony's relationships with his subordinates. Caesar remains aloof, a characteristic that was earlier apparent in his disdain for the drunken celebrations on board Pompey's galley and his distaste at Antony's association with 'knaves that smell of sweat' (I.4.21). Feasting appears routine amongst Antony and his men, but in Caesar's

[margin note:] Critical of both Ceasar & Antony

camp it only occurs when 'we have store to do't', and his soldiers 'have earned the waste' (IV.1.15–16). The deserters from Antony's camp are not made welcome but received with suspicion and hostility: Alexas persuades Herod to join with him in switching allegiance to Caesar and, as Enobarbus reports, 'For this pains/ Caesar hath hanged him' (IV.6.15–16). He is equally ruthless in his treatment of Antony and Cleopatra. He rejects Antony's request to live as a private man in Athens and makes it plain that he wishes him dead. He assures Cleopatra that he intends her 'no shame' (V.1.62) but in fact plans to humiliate her by displaying her as his captive in Rome.

Caesar is not an automaton but emotion is never allowed to interfere with the efficient exercise of power. His concern for Octavia's welfare appears sincere but it does not prevent her use as part of a political strategy. Moreover, his warning to Antony suggests that he regards Octavia primarily as an extension of himself: 'You take from me a great part of myself;/ Use me well in't' (III.2.24–25). Similarly, when she returns to Rome, his most immediate concern is that 'Caesar's sister' should have arrived with more ceremony and ostentation (III.6.42ff). His expressions of regret at the change in Antony also seem genuine (I.4), as do his tears at the news of Antony's death (V.1), but he quickly recovers his composure in the latter scene in order to return to official business — when a messenger from Cleopatra arrives, he tells his followers he will finish what he had been saying 'at some meeter season' (V.1.49). By the close of the scene he is already acting to ensure that sympathy for Antony does not damage his own position. He claims that he has documentary proof of his reluctance to engage in war.

The other character in *Antony and Cleopatra* with his sights set on political power is Pompey, who when he first appears in the play is confident that 'I shall do well' (II.1.8). In the same scene he shows an impressive insight into the characters of the triumvirs: Caesar 'gets money where/ He loses hearts', Antony is an 'amorous surfeiter' who is nevertheless to be feared because 'His soldiership/ Is twice the other twain' (II.1.13–14, 33–5). He is also perceptive enough to realise that in the face of his challenge any conflicts between the triumvirs will be temporarily put aside: 'lesser enmities may give way to greater . . . the fear of us/ May cement their divisions' (II.1.43, 47–48). When Antony,

Caesar and Lepidus do present the united front he had anticipated, his challenge to their position quickly evaporates. He
gains little from the terms he is offered — Sicily and Sardinia
are to be his but in return he must rid the sea of pirates and
supply wheat to Rome — and his ready acceptance arouses
Menas's contempt:

> Thy father, Pompey, would ne'er have made this treaty.
>
> (II.6.82–83)

It is Menas who in the galley scene offers to make Pompey 'lord
of all the world' by slitting the throats of the triumvirs (II.7.61).
Pompey's response indicates the hollowness of the Roman 'honour'
which he says forces him to reject Menas's proposal: he would
have happily approved of the murders and enjoyed the fruits of
the crime if Menas had only acted without consulting him.
Menas's decision, after Pompey's rejection of his offer, to 'never
follow thy palled fortunes more' (II.7.81) foreshadows, like
Enobarbus's later desertion of Antony, the downfall of his master.
Having wrested the initiative from Pompey by persuading him
to make peace with the triumvirate, Caesar soon mounts a fresh
offensive against him. After his defeat he is himself the victim of
assassination, at the hands of one of Antony's officers.

Caesar, then, is indisputably the play's supreme political
operator and by its close he stands alone and unchallenged, 'Sole
sir o'th'world' (V.2.120). Yet, impressive as Caesar's political
intelligence and acumen are, we are left with the feeling that
mediocrity has triumphed. It is a feeling common in Shakespeare's plays — one that accompanies, for example, the victory
of Malcolm in *Macbeth* and the accession to the throne of
Denmark of Fortinbras in *Hamlet*. Shakespeare compels us to
recognise Caesar's political mastery but also his human inadequacy.

AFTERTHOUGHTS

1

What makes a good leader?

2

Do you think that Caesar knows that Antony's marriage to Octavia will not last (pages 23–24)?

3

Do you agree that *Antony and Cleopatra* leaves its audience with the feeling that 'mediocrity has triumphed' (page 26)?

4

Do you feel that the argument of this essay suffers from omitting any consideration of Cleopatra's role?

Peter Hollindale

Peter Hollindale is Senior Lecturer in English and Education at the University of York. He is General Editor of the Macmillan Shakespeare, and has published numerous books and articles.

ESSAY

Music under the earth: the suicide marriage in *Antony and Cleopatra*

Although there is reference to augurers and divinations, only one incident in *Antony and Cleopatra* is explicitly supernatural. It comes in Act IV scene 3, after Antony has disgraced his honour and ruined his cause by fleeing from the sea-battle in pursuit of Cleopatra. The soldiers are keeping watch over Antony's camp by night when there is (stage direction): *Music of hautboys under the stage.* This dialogue then follows:

> SECOND SOLDIER   Peace! What noise?
> FIRST SOLDIER   List, list!
> SECOND SOLDIER   Hark!
> FIRST SOLDIER   Music i'th'air.
> THIRD SOLDIER   Under the earth.
> FOURTH SOLDIER   It signs well, does it not?
> THIRD SOLDIER   No.
> FIRST SOLDIER   Peace, I say!
>   What should this mean?
> SECOND SOLDIER   'Tis the god Hercules, whom Antony loved,
>   Now leaves him.
>
>   (IV.3.13–18)

This strange episode has its origin in Shakespeare's source for the play, the chronicles of Plutarch, but Shakespeare has made certain changes in its nature and its timing. In Plutarch it is Bacchus, god of wine and revelry, who makes a sinister and timely exit from the falling hero's company. In Shakespeare it is Hercules, supposedly Antony's ancestor and the archetypal figure of godlike strength and courage. In Plutarch the deserter is a patron god, and one who stood for those disorderly and hedonistic temptations which have ruined Antony's career. In Shakespeare the departing shade is one who mirrors the superhuman qualities of Antony, and stands astride the boundary line between man and god. The change is fully in keeping with Shakespeare's Antony, and Shakespeare's play, and with the ambiguities of status and of fate on which its tragic outcome depends.

Undeniably the incident is an ominous one, yet it can be understood in more than one way, even hopefully. ('It signs well, does it not?') The soldiers are troubled and disturbed, but uncertain. Music is strange and untimely in the threatening night, but it is made from concords of sound. They are not even sure where it is, in the air or under the earth. If under the earth, it suggests death, burial, dissolution, vacancy; if in the air, it suggests disappearance, escape, freedom. If Hercules, not Bacchus, is departing, it suggests the liberation of the immortal from confines which have pushed mortality to its limit. An occurrence which is chiefly ominous is in part transcendent.

The change of godlike presence and the timing of the scene cause subtle changes in the status of Antony, and their effect is to ennoble him. Rather than the revelries of Bacchus, whom in both Plutarch and Shakespeare 'in the manner of his life he followed', he is joined instead — albeit in defeat and ending — with the warlike godliness of Hercules. The shift of emphasis confirms the effect of scenes which precede and follow this one. In Act III scene 13, and in Act IV scene 2, in the aftermath of dishonour and defeat, Antony has repeatedly summoned his followers to feasting:

> Let's have one other gaudy night. Call to me
> All my sad captains. Fill our bowls once more.
> Let's mock the midnight bell.

(III.13.182–184)

>   Let's tonight
>   Be bounteous at our meal.

(IV.2.9–10)

This desperate revelry in the face of calamity causes distress to his loyal followers, and might be viewed as perverse and irresponsible self-consolation. But in between the two scenes of summoning to misplaced prodigality comes Act IV scene 1, and Caesar's chill and frugal equivalent:

>   And feast the army; we have store to do't,
>   And they have earned the waste.

(IV.1.15–16)

The contrast is too plain to be accidental; and the effect is to place the emphasis not on Antony's wastefulness, his irresponsible taste for pleasure and gluttony, his soldierly negligence, but on his magnanimity, his affection for those who are loyal to him, his instinct for ceremonious fellowship, and his bravery in affirming life-values to the end. These are not the coarse Egyptian bacchanals of earlier scenes, but the festive rituals of war. It is indeed Hercules, not Bacchus, for whom Antony is performing appropriate last rites before the end.

The other significant change which Shakespeare made was to follow the supernatural episode by Antony's last, brief military success before he is finally conquered. In Plutarch the ominous event of Bacchus's departure is followed immediately by the fleet's desertion and surrender, but in Shakespeare there is one final glimpse of the Herculean Antony before his fortunes are irrevocably destroyed. This too has its place in the emergent pattern of the death-scenes. Throughout the play we have seen in Antony (as in Cleopatra also) an incongruous partnership of youth and age in the same body, a part-heroic, part-absurd refusal to admit the loss of youth and onset of age, either in themselves or in each other. In despair and disgrace after fleeing from Caesar's ships, Antony bitterly sums up this self-division, taking as its symptom the mingled colours of his hair:

>   My very hairs do mutiny, for the white
>   Reprove the brown for rashness, and they them
>   For fear and doting.

(III.11.13–15)

After this last victorious skirmish, he returns to the idea, but differently. He is now accepting the erosion of youthfulness by time, yet still laying heroic claims to compete with youth on equal terms:

> What, girl! Though grey
> Do something mingle with our younger brown, yet ha' we
> A brain that nourishes our nerves, and can
> Get goal for goal of youth.

(IV.8.19–22)

This scene becomes a step towards the transformation and transcendence which accompany the suicide and death of the closing scenes, the recovery of life and youth beyond death, the world inhabited by the 'curlèd Antony' with whom Cleopatra seeks reunion outside the reach of earthbound Caesardom.

The disappearance of Hercules in this enigmatic little scene is therefore a considered shift in the play's imaginative centre. It is indeed ominous, because no reprieve can now halt Antony's destruction, but it also introduces ideas which are crucial to the deaths of Antony and Cleopatra themselves: ideas of immortality and godlikeness, of escape and vanishing, of ceasing to be earthbound. It also raises the status of Antony, turning us away from the acts and omissions which have degraded him in Roman eyes, and towards the Herculean standing which will make him a fit partner beyond death for Cleopatra. In their imagined after-world, beyond suicide, lies the rejuvenated vision of marriage which life itself will not allow them.

The dramatic presentation of Antony raises a problem for Shakespeare which the presentation of Cleopatra does not. In the theatre the problem is simply that Antony dies so early, and he must 'survive' theatrically as a memory and an image of sufficient power to sustain his equality with the Queen in the closing scenes. Earlier in the play he is at a disadvantage also. Cleopatra (as Enobarbus memorably points out) is impressive even when she is undignified, whether resplendent in the barge at Cydnus or hopping forty paces through the public street. She is a pattern of vibrant female life, wholly at home in her own place, so that Egypt is an extension of her own persona. She can fashion life, and love-in-life, in her own image, and in the transcendent final act she can do the same to death itself.

Antony, by contrast, is a traitor to the standards and values by which the world judges him, an ignoble self-reducer, 'The triple pillar of the world transformed/ Into a strumpet's fool.' No longer in charge of his own life, his very presence in Egypt, and still more his return to it, constitute a helpless self-abasement, a denial of power and duty and responsibility and honour and contract, perhaps a denial of 'reality' itself. Almost exactly half the play depicts his incompetent losing of a war, and the consequence of that; the first half shows us the process of political ineptitude which brings the war upon him in the first place.

For Shakespeare to make us feel, as he does, that the tragedy of Antony and Cleopatra is a double tragedy of love, a tragedy of equals, and that a transcendent act of mutual imagination can turn their tragedy into something which is also a triumph, calls for much dramatic skill and subtlety. Taking the 'supernatural' scene of Hercules's leavetaking as a key example, I have tried to show some of the ways in which this is accomplished at a crucial stage of the action. Shakespeare's dramatic exposition must include three things. First, he must show Antony in situations of undignified belittlement, because plot and circumstances dictate it, and he must show them as compatible with retained, indeed enhanced, heroic stature. Second, he must show the interdependence, the indivisibility of Antony and Cleopatra, so that the inevitability of their relationship — which in life can be dismissed as mere seductiveness on one side, and craven servitude on the other — is tested beyond destruction by defeat and death. Third, he must induce us to accept a changed imaginative valuation of life and death themselves.

During the battle scenes, the phase of action which includes Hercules's leavetaking, the first of these is achieved. The faults which brought Antony to destruction — helpless infatuation, sensuality, absenteeism and neglect of duty, profligacy, self-indulgence — are shown in the last phase of their ruinous progression displaced by kindred qualities which impress us — fidelity in love, magnanimity, generosity, festive gratitude, defiance. He is still a deeply flawed man, as Cleopatra is a deeply flawed woman, but things which show ignobly in the everyday commerce of life become transfigured by the imminence and fact of death.

The second and third of the dramatic problems I have

outlined depend entirely on the fact of suicide and our response to the idea of escape. Crucial to Shakespeare's resolution of his dramatic needs is the idea of mutuality, culminating as it does (in visionary imagination at least) in the ultimate mutuality of immortal marriage.

Suicide is pre-eminently a Roman act, and its associations are with courage and honour in the face of defeat. A cluster of Roman concepts surrounds it, which we can see in the Act IV scenes of Antony's suicide. Avoidance of public disgrace is perhaps the most important. Antony depicts it graphically to Eros:

> Wouldst thou be windowed in great Rome and see
> Thy master thus: with pleached arms, bending down
> His corrigible neck, his face subdued
> To penetrative shame, whilst the wheeled seat
> Of fortunate Caesar, drawn before him, branded
> His baseness that ensued?

> (IV.14.72–77)

The dominant motive is not to avoid punishment and retribution, or to avoid a more painful death, but to avoid humiliation, and especially the humiliation of being made into a public spectacle for vulgar crowds to boggle at. Along with this goes the desire to seize a kind of conquest even in the presence of defeat. Roman suicide includes the idea of self-conquest, and the belief that by ending one's own life, voluntarily, one deprives the conqueror of victory and regains the victory for oneself. Believing that Cleopatra is dead, Antony blames himself for showing less courage and nobility than:

> . . . she which by her death our Caesar tells
> 'I am conqueror of myself.'

> (IV.14.61–62)

One step further on in the logic of honourable suicide is the notion that to end one's own life inflicts an overthrow on one's conqueror, as Antony declares when he tells Eros, ''tis Caesar thou defeat'st'.

These ideas are the nucleus of Roman suicide, and in expressing them at his death Antony is finally showing himself the complete and sufficient Roman, despite all that went before. But what we notice most strikingly in the play is the adoption of these same ideas by Cleopatra. In one short passage, just before Antony dies, we hear unmistakably the mutuality of their ideas:

> ANTONY Not Caesar's valour hath o'erthrown Antony,
> But Antony's hath triumphed on itself.
> CLEOPATRA So it should be, that none but Antony
> Should conquer Antony, but woe 'tis so!
>
> (IV.15.14–17)

Shortly after his death, she aligns herself courageously with the values of Roman suicide, in what is effectively a posthumous marriage of Roman idealism:

> We'll bury him; and then, what's brave, what's noble,
> Let's do't after the high Roman fashion,
> And make death proud to take us.
>
> (IV.15.85–87)

Thereafter, throughout Act V, Cleopatra's complex movement towards suicide repeatedly includes these selfsame objects and priorities that Antony affirmed. She too fears more than anything the humiliation of public captivity, and the prospect of being shown off in triumph to 'the shouting varletry/ Of censuring Rome'. She too fears the prospect of imposed, compulsory humility in the proud and chastening presence of those she has offended: she will not 'be chastised with the sober eye/ Of dull Octavia'. Suicide is honourable prevention of these nightmares. Cleopatra too regards suicide as a noble internalising of control over fate, an act of heroic self-sufficiency in a hostile world:

> He words me, girls, he words me, that I should not
> Be noble to myself.
>
> (V.2.191–192)

and one which removes the spoils of conquest from the victor:

> This mortal house I'll ruin,
> Do Caesar what he can.
>
> (V.2.51–52)

And Cleopatra too takes the final logical step of supposing that the act of suicide transforms the enemy's victory into defeat. As she applies the asp to her breast, she says to it:

> O, couldst thou speak,
> That I might hear thee call great Caesar ass
> Unpolicied!

(V.2.305–307)

In short, the terms of Roman suicide are nobly fulfilled in the mutuality and reflexive nature of the lovers' deaths, as Cleopatra adopts and meets the highest demands of Antony's Romanness.

But this is only part of the story. The Roman part of it concerns the disposal of a life which has become unlivable in honour because of conquest and defeat. However, for both the lovers the immediate impulse to suicide comes not from Caesar's victory but from knowledge of the other's death. Antony's 'knowledge' is of course illusory — it stems from the ruses of the living Cleopatra as we know her, a woman who is deceitful, wily and self-preserving — but its effects are none the less authentic for that. It is essential to the play's dramatic effect that we should see each of them reacting to the death of the other, and only illusion can permit it (as it does in *Romeo and Juliet*). The effect is broadly the same on each of them: a heavy and exhausted sense that meaningful life is over and the world is stale and pointless. It is bereavement within the Egyptian world of love, not military conquest, which is the primary driving force to suicide. The sense of mortal relaxation, and futility in all possible effort, is strong in Antony's lines:

> All length is torture; since the torch is out,
> Lie down, and stray no farther. Now all labour
> Mars what it does; yea, very force entangles
> Itself with strength. Seal then, and all is done.

(IV.14.46–49)

Antony's lines and mood — like his body later, as he is lifted to Cleopatra's monument — have the physical heaviness of the exhausted soldier. Cleopatra's equivalent lines are appropriately lighter in tone, but their wistful elegiac quietness records the same irrevocable sense of collapsed significance in all things:

> O, withered is the garland of the war,
> The soldier's pole is fall'n; young boys and girls

Are level now with men. The odds is gone,
And there is nothing left remarkable
Beneath the visiting moon.

(IV.15.64–68)

In the awareness of death, all the varied world is reduced to nothing compared with the newly exalted singleness of value that each has for the other. Suicide therefore becomes the only possible and tolerable act, and its performance becomes effectively indistinguishable from marriage.

In the last phase of the play, therefore, suicide becomes an ambiguous action, betokening both the extinction of a life and also the *dispersal* of life to a new and protected immortality where neither Caesar nor any other earthly bond can capture and confine it. It is an action, but also a *process*, of transcendent change, escape, disappearance and renewal. There is an end, but also a continuum.

The play has its own distinctive vocabulary to denote the process of dispersal. The central word in it is 'melt', a word which occurs repeatedly. The vocabulary is a neutral one: by no means all its connotations are favourable or pleasant, but it steadily reinforces a fundamental imaginative concept, that of solid substances liquefying or turning into air and vapour. The world of the play is one which is forever losing its tactile firmness, and metamorphosing into more indistinct, elusive elements. Apart from the reiterated 'melt', other words in the group include 'dissolve', 'discandy', 'disponge', 'dislimns'. Their cumulative effect is one of instability, which can in varying circumstances be either harmful or protective.

One of the effects of this distinctive verbal group is to strengthen the imaginative unifying of Antony and Cleopatra, to affirm their indivisibility. Each of them uses it. When Cleopatra is denying Antony's accusations of coldness, she calls for her neck to be penetrated by poisoned hail if she is so:

> as it determines, so
> Dissolve my life! The next Caesarion smite,
> Till by degrees the memory of my womb,
> Together with my brave Egyptians all,
> By the discandying of this pelleted storm,
> Lie graveless . . .

(III.13.161–166)

Antony, complaining of Cleopatra's treachery and that of his followers, declares:

> The hearts
> That spanieled me at heels, to whom I gave
> Their wishes, do discandy, melt their sweets
> On blossoming Caesar

(IV.12.20–23)

In these two passages Antony and Cleopatra have in common a rare and distinct vocabulary which expresses the same idea of liquefaction. Both imagine the people who made up the human sweetness of their lives — offspring and subjects, comrades and followers — as dissolving away from them in the over-sweetness of corruption. Each is left with a sense of solitude and personal dissolution, yet the language itself has the effect of binding them together in a shared and inseparable plight.

However, the vocabulary of dispersal has positive values too, associated initially with disappearance and then with escape and freedom. The transformative action of the closing scenes of the play has the effect of converting ideas of negative repugnance into ideas of affirmative triumph, in a similar process to that which converted Antony's negative Egyptian dissoluteness into nobler values compatible equally with Egypt and with Rome. We can see such a moment of change in Act IV scene 14, where Antony is talking to Eros about the illusory substance and instability of cloud-shapes:

> That which is now a horse, even with a thought
> The rack dislimns, and makes it indistinct
> As water is in water.

(IV.14.9–11)

He links this, in a mood of sad revulsion, with himself, in what he takes to be his solitary, ruined and deserted state: the material Antony of his mortal life no longer exists:

> Here I am Antony,
> Yet cannot hold this visible shape, my knave.

(IV.14.13–14)

Yet the final effect of the play is to transform this hurtful image of dispersal into the very basis of escape, reunion and triumph. Even perceived in grief, at the moment of death, the suicidal bridge to another world becomes an imperceptible move to a celestial place of immortal life, recovered youth, and untouchable safety. As Antony dies, 'The crown o'th'earth doth *melt*'. When Iras dies, Cleopatra takes her gentle expiring as a sign of the world's worthlessness, and the verb she uses, 'vanish', is important:

> If thus thou vanishest, thou tell'st the world
> It is not worth leave-taking.

> (V.2.296–297)

and Cleopatra's words for her own death, in the moments of its happening, are 'As sweet as balm, as soft as air, as gentle'.

There is in fact a unity of echoes in the language and experience of Antony and Cleopatra in these closing scenes which composes a complex image of marital oneness, and the process of suicide, the ideas and acts associated with it, are inseparable from this unity. Even the image of youthful and impulsive haste in dying, making of it a lyrical and sensuous burst of refuge-seeking, is one that they share:

> ANTONY   But I will be
> A bridegroom in my death, and run into't
> As to a lover's bed.

> (IV.14.99–101)

> CLEOPATRA   then is it sin
> To rush into the secret house of death
> Ere death dare come to us?

> (IV.15.79–81)

As they prepare for their chosen suicides, there is an explicit impulse towards revived youth and marital reunion with the dead partner. In both their cases it is personal, impetuous and free, a renunciation before death of the constricting world they are leaving:

> ANTONY   Eros! — I come, my queen — Eros! Stay for me.
> Where souls do couch on flowers, we'll hand in hand,
> And with our sprightly port make the ghosts gaze

> (IV.14.50–52)

CLEOPATRA   Husband, I come.
Now to that name my courage prove my title!
I am fire and air; my other elements
I give to baser life.

(V.2.286–289)

Even the balance of these twin speeches reflects their final mutuality in love; each of them is spontaneously generous, subordinating self to the values and status of the partner. Antony's avowal is in terms of love, the quality of Egypt, and he salutes Cleopatra by the royal title from which the victories of imperial Rome have effectively deposed her. Cleopatra claims Antony as 'Husband', thereby setting aside the formalities of division and estrangement which his alliances with Fulvia and Octavia have earlier caused, and her avowal is in terms of courage, the prized quality of Rome.

The imaginative vision of reunion (whether illusory or not) is indisputable in these scenes. I have tried to show that it is a part of a complex pattern of associations which cumulatively reinforces its power, including certain ambiguities of vocabulary and dramatic effect which enable the drama to take on its unique transformative quality. The enigmatic scene of Hercules's departure is one such ambiguity. In one way it registers Antony's downfall, symbolising the Herculean hero's reduction to the ruined man; but in another it anticipates the process of momentous death and disappearance which Antony himself will follow, vanishing underground or into the shifting vaporous clouds, and leaving Caesar with only earth itself as empire. Of the four elements, earth, air, fire and water, Caesar is left behind as undisputed master of the earth alone.

I have also suggested that the transformative process is inseparable from the rituals of suicide. In these, both Rome and Egypt have their place, with Antony and Cleopatra finding in self-inflicted death a fusion of their two worlds which proved disastrously impossible to achieve in life. Yet to depict the play as even-handed in its final effect would in my view be mistaken. Before his suicide, Antony disarms himself. Exhausted by war, he puts aside for ever the uniform of Rome. Before her suicide, Cleopatra dresses, reassuming the robes and crown of her Egyptian dignity. In so far as the play dramatises the collision of two incompatible worlds, this detail — more powerful on stage than in the printed text — seems accurately to embody its imaginative verdict.

AFTERTHOUGHTS

1

What reasons does Hollindale suggest for the changes Shakespeare has made to his source material in depicting the leave-taking of Hercules?

2

Does the audience's memory of Antony, after his death in Act IV, '"survive" theatrically...to sustain his equality with the Queen in the closing scenes' (page 31)?

3

If Antony's and Cleopatra's suicides constitute a transcendant marriage, can the play fairly be viewed as a tragedy?

4

What 'imaginative verdict' is suggested to you by the two details cited by Hollindale in the final paragraph of this essay?

Graham Holderness
*Graham Holderness is Head of the
Drama Department at the Roehampton
Institute, and has published numerous
works of criticism.*

ESSAY

'Some squeaking Cleopatra': theatricality in *Antony and Cleopatra*

> Now, Iras, what think'st thou?
> Thou, an Egyptian puppet shall be shown
> In Rome as well as I. Mechanic slaves
> With greasy aprons, rules, and hammers shall
> Uplift us to the view. In their thick breaths,
> Rank of gross diet, shall we be enclouded,
> And forced to drink their vapour.
>   . . .
>   Saucy lictors
> Will catch at us like strumpets, and scald rhymers
> Ballad us out o'tune. The quick comedians
> Extemporally will stage us, and present
> Our Alexandrian revels. Antony
> Shall be brought drunken forth, and I shall see
> Some squeaking Cleopatra boy my greatness
> I'th'posture of a whore.

>   (5.2.207–221)

Antony is dead, his forces routed; Egypt is conquered, Caesar's star is in the ascendant. Cleopatra squarely confronts the natural destiny of the defeated: to be led through the streets of Rome at Caesar's chariot wheels. In an earlier speech, after Cleopatra's flight from the battle of Actium, Antony threatened her with such ritual humiliation as the inevitable wages of defeat:

> Vanish, or I shall give thee thy deserving
> And blemish Caesar's triumph. Let him take thee
> And hoist thee up to the shouting plebeians;
> Follow his chariot, like the greatest spot
> Of all thy sex; most monster-like be shown
> For poor'st diminutives . . .

(IV.12.32–37)

Although they are talking about precisely the same eventuality, Antony and Cleopatra describe it in significantly different ways. Antony, statesman and soldier, imagines the scene almost entirely in political and military terms: what Cleopatra should fear (and what, in his anger, he enjoys threatening her with) is the shame and humiliation of greatness humbled and military power subdued. Caesar will 'hoist' Cleopatra up before the Roman plebeians, exhibit her to the populace as a trophy of the Emperor's military success; he will draw her in chains after his chariot, the most degraded of women; show her to the meanest of people ('poor'st diminutives') like the 'monster' of a travelling freak-show.

Cleopatra's imaginary dramatisation of the same scene is both more specific, and more complex in its range of references. Antony's undifferentiated crowd of 'shouting plebeians' resolves in Cleopatra's imagination into sharper focus, a crowd of 'mechanic slaves' (labourers) bearing the tools and uniforms of their trades — 'greasy aprons, rules, and hammers'. The Queen's aristocratic disgust focuses with physical repugnance on the 'thick breaths' and 'gross diet' of the common people to whose mockery she and Iras will be subjected. It is not only, however, the enforced physical proximity to that repulsive mob that concerns Cleopatra: she will, she fears, be treated as one of them, as a common 'strumpet' (prostitute) arrested and subjected to the discipline of the lictors (magistrates). She will be punished, then, not only for her resistance to the power of imperial Rome, but for her lascivious reputation as Antony's lover: her sexuality as well as her political power will be humiliated.

Despoiled for her greatness, political authority, royal majesty, she will be regarded as little more than a common criminal. But an awareness of that former greatness will of course still be there: the enjoyment of the mob is not in the disciplining of a common whore, but in the ritual subjection of a foreign empress. Cleopatra's greatness will be displayed in Rome in the form of parodic performances, improvised street-entertainments, puppet-shows, mocking ballads and scurrilous rhymes. She and Antony, great heroic figures of an epic destiny, will appear presented in the parodic mockery of popular entertainment. Actors ('comedians' means comedy actors rather than stand-up comics — though the context suggests that the two concepts could be closely related here) will portray them on stage, Antony played as a farcical drunk, Cleopatra performed — according to Elizabethan stage practice — by a boy, whose 'squeaking' voice will ridicule the legendary eminence of the former empress of Egypt.

Cleopatra's vision of defeat thus operates on several different levels. Her greatness will be humbled, her subdued power displayed. She will be exhibited as an instance of Caesar's power. The ritual humiliation of Caesar's triumph will subject her to the mockery of the mob, and reduce her to their social status. She will be mocked not only as a conquered rebel, but also as a notorious whore. Lastly, her former greatness will be imitated in satirical popular shows, her majesty subversively enacted by common players, her romantic legend scurrilously mocked by the broad humour of street-entertainers. Degradation, sexual humiliation, imitation: the three primary terms of her imagined shame merge together in these concluding words, as Cleopatra predicts the manner of her theatrical representation:

> Some squeaking Cleopatra boy my greatness
> I'th'posture of a whore.

(V.2.220–221)

Both her greatness and her sexuality will be negated, as she is imitated on stage by a common player in the 'squeaking' voice of a mere boy.

* * *

The Globe Theatre, on London's Bankside, 1607. I have paid a penny to stand among the spectators in the yard of the famous theatre, watching a performance of Antony and Cleopatra. *When the actor playing Antony delivers that threatening speech predicting the shames of defeat, I can feel his anger, feel Cleopatra's fear. As he describes the projected scene of Caesar's triumph in Rome, I can picture, through the actor's shouted fury, the imagined event — Roman streets, chariots, shouting plebeians. Antony seems just about to strike Cleopatra when she dashes out of one of the rear doors, desperate to escape her lover's ungovernable rage. In the excitement conjured up by the actor's emotional intensity, I never for a moment lost my imaginative sense that I was watching a historical figure, the great Antony, possessed by the genuine anguish of his tragic destiny. Not for a second did the illusion of the theatre loosen its grip on me: I am not here in a theatre in London, but in Alexandria or Rome, in a fictional world of epic event and legendary action.*

The actor playing Cleopatra is a boy, but that is not something that disturbs my enjoyment or concentration as a spectator: on the contrary, it would seem strange to me if it were otherwise. The female costume, the vivid facial make-up and the wig effectively disguise the actor's gender, and his unbroken voice approximates closely enough to the female pitch. I am quite happy to accept him as presenting the legendary Queen of Egypt. When Cleopatra delivers her speech predicting Caesar's triumph, the dramatic mood is quite different. She knows the worst, and her tone is thoughtful, reflective. 'Thou, an Egyptian puppet' . . . does she mean that the pretty doll-like Iras will be exhibited as a toy, or that someone will make a puppet to resemble her? There was a puppet-show going on outside the theatre when I came in . . . 'Mechanic slaves/ With greasy aprons, rules, and hammers' . . . Cleopatra could be talking about this audience — look, there's a cobbler, taking the afternoon off to go the theatre, wearing just such a greasy apron, his hammer slung in his belt . . . 'thick breaths' . . . God, I know just what she means, this apprentice next to me's eating a raw onion . . . 'strumpets', there are plenty of those here, not Roman ones though . . . 'The quick comedians/ Extemporally will stage us' . . . but that's just what's happening now, there on that stage ... 'some squeaking Cleopatra boy my greatness' ... of course, the actor is a boy, I recognise him now, underneath all that paint, he played the Fool yesterday ... and today he's Cleopatra!

* * *

When we see Shakespeare performed today, we *normally* see the plays in a theatrical environment where actors strive to represent real life as naturally as possible (and so would be unlikely to use a man to play Cleopatra), and where the audience is prepared for a special 'cultural' occasion, dressed for leisure rather than for work, and dressed *alike* — glancing around a theatre audience at the interval, you wouldn't immediately be able to distinguish the plumber from the chartered accountant, the teacher from the nurse. Our awareness of those fellow-spectators is in any case diminished in the modern theatre by the convention of the darkened auditorium, the brightly illuminated stage. Or we might be watching the play in a film or television version, with the audience eliminated from the space of the performance altogether. A traditional modern theatre isolates the dramatic event from other kinds of experience: eating and drinking are confined to the bar, while the street outside is likely to be full of traffic rather than street-entertainers.

All these factors governing the nature of modern theatrical performance would conspire to minimise the differences between those two speeches, between Antony and Cleopatra as each imagines the likely outcome of their defeat. In each case the actor would simply be constructing an imaginary vision of a probable outcome, and describing it for us to see: Cleopatra's might seem more vivid, but neither speech would break out of the sharply delineated performance space into which the modern theatre confines it. In the kind of Jacobean theatre in which *Antony and Cleopatra* would have been produced, perhaps in 1607, the two speeches would have worked quite differently, by virtue of very different conditions and contexts of performance. The audience was both mixed and clearly diversified: a person's trade or profession was immediately obvious from his/her appearance, and the audience in a Jacobean public playhouse would have contained many spectators who had more in common with Antony's 'plebeians' than with the queens and triumvirs who populated the stage.

Since all performances took place in daylight, members of the audience would have been much more aware of one another than in a modern theatre. The theatre would have stood, as did the Globe, in a locality particularly devoted to popular entertainment — shows of all kinds, bear-baiting, cock-fighting, fencing displays, juggling, tumbling — and the satisfaction of popular appetites — taverns, eating houses, brothels. Food and drink were sold and consumed within the theatre building. On the stage itself, the actors did not aim consistently at the creation of dramatic illusion: boys played women, the stage itself had no scenery or other means of representing location. Actors could seek to draw their audience into a theatrical illusion, or break that illusion, whenever they wanted to, or whenever the dramatic text they were performing permitted.

Thus when Antony talks of Caesar's triumph, the attention of the Jacobean audience would have been on the actor's portrayal of a character's emotions, and on the picture he paints in words of Cleopatra's humiliation. When Cleopatra depicts the same scene, her theatrical discourse functions in a much more complex way. She (or he on the Jacobean stage) draws the attention of the audience away from the fictional world of the drama, the imagined Rome or Alexandria of the spectator's suspended disbelief, and towards the material conditions surrounding the performance itself. Cleopatra's speech actively reminds the audience that the actor is not the Queen of Egypt, but a boy player; that the fear expressed by these historical characters of theatrical imitation has already overtaken them, since they are being played by actors now, at this very moment; that the very existence of the theatrical illusion that allows a boy to mimic Cleopatra depends precisely on the willingness of that mixed audience of modern-day 'plebeians', for whose Roman ancestors the historical character has nothing but contempt.

How then would this continual breaking of theatrical illusion have operated on the spectators? Would they be disappointed, all enjoyment spoiled? Would they demand their money back, regarding the spectacle of a boy dressed as a woman as hardly worth a hard-earned penny? Would they walk out of the theatre, disgusted at the poverty disclosed by these devices of disen-chantment? Our modern prejudices in favour of naturalism in acting and dramatic production may dispose us to feel that a broken illusion is a worthless instrument, damaged beyond repair. Yet in fact this deliberate suspension of illusion, which Brecht called 'alienation-effect', is not in any sense incompatible with enjoyment, with full imaginative participation by the audi-ence, or indeed with the immediate reconstruction of the dra-matic illusion itself.

Cleopatra's speech provides an example of the extraordinary richness and vitality of Jacobean theatrical language. The play can construct a convincing simulation of a historical reality, put history on the stage and make us believe it. It can also rupture the illusion of that dramatised fiction, thus calling the attention of the audience to the mechanisms by which the illusion is constructed. At these moments, the substance of the drama does not remain isolated and cut off inside a charmed circle of dramatic verisimilitude: instead it is thrown into an exciting interaction with the complex and varied facts of the spectator's everyday life. The world outside the theatre is connected to the imagined world constructed within it; and above all the active participation of the theatrical audience is acknowledged as a co-author of the dramatic illusion itself. Through the mediation of the boy actor, Cleopatra and the craftsman with the greasy apron who stands in the yard of the Globe theatre suddenly, momentarily, occupy the same dimension of space and time: though their co-existence is simultaneously fissured by a clear awareness of the provisional and artificial nature of this tem-porary synthesis.

The continual implicit comparison invoked by these 'meta-dramatic' effects, between the great public figures of history, and the actors who represent them, can work in two opposite directions. In one perspective, the legendary reputations of the heroic past are diminished, degraded by theatrical imitation; performed by and to people of enormously lower status, their nobility is subverted, their epic virtues ridiculed and mocked. Paradoxically, Elizabethan and Jacobean plays that were per-formed daily to a popular audience, by actors whose social status could be regarded as little higher than that of the beggar or the criminal, are full of slighting references to the baseness of their own audiences, and to the pettiness of their own performers. One famous example is to be found in Hamlet's observations about acting and theatre: where the popular audience is stigmatised as crude and stupid, 'capable of nothing but dumb-shows and inexplicable noise', while the actor is categorised as a kind of prostitute, paid to speak words he does not mean, hired to simulate emotions he does not feel.

Yet in the very same scene Hamlet acknowledges that actors can also claim great power and responsibility. For it is their craftsmanship, properly exercised, that can 'hold the mirror up to nature', and 'show the very age her form and pressure'. Dramatic representation is clearly not reality or truth: but its extraordinary capacity for securing illusion makes it a powerful means of impersonating reality, simulating truth. And that power applies as much to the personages of the great and eminent, as to more mundane levels of reality: in fact of course, as Hamlet half-acknowledges by comparing himself to an actor, the noble Prince Hamlet himself can appear on a stage only when one of those despised players comes forward to represent him.

And this is the other perspective invoked by the theatrical representation of greatness: if actors can convincingly impress an audience with the charisma of nobility, the aura of power, then perhaps actors may share to some degree in that charisma, in that power. Perhaps there is something in common between the performers in the theatre, and the kings, queens, princes they play. Are not kings, queens and princes, after all, performers in a different kind of drama, the theatre of public life? In a culture where political authority habitually manifested and authorised itself by elaborate ritual displays of magnificence and majesty, what is the king but an actor in a carefully stage-managed performance? This feature of Elizabethan/Jacobean drama constitutes one aspect of what was considered at the time to be its dangerousness. Political authority in this historical period relied on pretensions to 'natural' authority, either acquired by royal and noble birth, or granted by divine appointment. It could be somewhat dangerous to admit that power could in fact be *acted*, since to acknowledge power as a display opened up the possibility of seeing it as artificial rather than natural, imposed rather than organic.

This brings us back to *Antony and Cleopatra*. The fate Cleopatra sketches for herself as Caesar's captive never, of course, occurs. Instead she succeeds in cheating her conqueror, manages after all to 'blemish Caesar's triumph'. The method she uses is that of suicide. Suicide in this play can appear as merely an escape, from intolerable circumstances, or as a personal triumph, an apotheosis. We have already witnessed one suicide, that of Antony. His suicide is of course bungled, doesn't even work properly: he succeeds only in mortally wounding himself, to die later. As he initially falls on his sword, he tries to capture some of Cleopatra's rich sensual poetry: 'I will be/ A bridegroom in my death, and run into't/ As to a lover's bed' (IV.14.99–101). But later, at the actual point of death, Antony has lost all positive sense of death as a goal to be sought, actively and with passion. Despite the Roman notion of suicide as a dignified and honourable course, Antony is more conscious of the 'miserable change' that has brought him to a humiliating death. 'Please your thoughts', he tells Cleopatra, 'In feeding them with those my former fortunes'/ Wherein I lived; the greatest prince o'th'world' (IV.15.52–54).

Cleopatra's suicide is, by contrast, a magnificently successful performance. Antony's use of the traditional Roman method, falling on the sword, was a clumsy failure. Cleopatra chooses to die by the bite of the asp, which is not only painless and certain, but calculated (as Caesar wonderingly acknowledges) to leave the corpse beautiful in death (see V.2.342–346). In her preparatory speech (Cleopatra prefers to deliver her own funeral oration in advance) the Queen reaffirms all those qualities Caesar's triumph would have humiliated: her majesty, her nobility, her sensuality:

> Give me my robe; put on my crown; I have
> Immortal longings in me.
> ...
> The stroke of death is as a lover's pinch,
> Which hurts, and is desired.
>
> (V.2.279–280, 294–295)

This triumphant restoration of the Queen in the full sensual majesty of her being, is a self-dramatisation, just as much a performance as Caesar's anticipated and deflected triumph would have been. But Cleopatra has taken control of her own destiny with such admirable firmness because she is fully prepared to embrace the dramatic, to put on a show, to re-establish through performance those qualities of which Caesar would have robbed her. What has happened to the boy actor who a few lines previously reminded us obtrusively of his existence? He has of course been incorporated into a self-dramatising legend, drawn up in the force of a theatrical passion, become all 'fire, and air': indistinguishable from Cleopatra. It is one thing to understand the nature of dramatic illusion: quite another to deny its power.

AFTERTHOUGHTS

1

What distinctions does Holderness draw between Antony's and Cleopatra's visions of public humiliation in Rome?

2

What is the function of the italicised section of this essay (pages 45–46)? How effective do you find it?

3

What do you understand by 'metadramatic' (page 48)?

4

'And this is the other perspective...' (page 49): what political argument is Holderness putting forward in this paragraph? Do you agree?

Michael Gearin-Tosh

Michael Gearin-Tosh is Fellow and Tutor in English Literature at St Catherine's College, Oxford. He is also Associate Director of the Oxford School of Drama.

ESSAY

Love in
Antony and Cleopatra

Cleopatra was a popular subject for drama before Shakespeare. Most authors, however, focused upon her suicide and their plays start after Antony's death or, if earlier, after his defeat at Actium. It is Shakespeare's greatness to show Antony and Cleopatra in love, in the celebration of their love before disaster strikes, and after it has struck. No doubt this was the point of his title: not *Cleopatra*, an Italian play of 1542, nor *Cléopatre Captive*, a French play of 1552, nor *The Tragedie of Cleopatra*, an English play of the 1590s — there were several others whose titles reflect different emphases — but a simple naming and coupling of the two lovers, *Antony and Cleopatra*.

The nature of their love is thrown into relief by how Shakespeare changed his source, the ancient writer Plutarch. Plutarch's Octavia is as beautiful as Cleopatra, younger, and possessed of 'an excellent grace, wisdom and honesty joined unto so rare a beauty'. Antony falls in love with her, their marriage lasts several years, there are children, and when Antony and Caesar first raise armies against each other, she successfully reconciles them. Compared to this, Shakespeare's Octavia is almost a cypher. She appears only three times with Antony. Each time she says farewell, and twice to him. Her 'holy, cold, and still conversation' (II.6.120–121) never stands a chance with Antony, as Enobarbus sees from the start.

This reduction of Octavia goes with a different time scheme. Her marriage lasts a couple of months, it seems, in Shakespeare. Plutarch, when Antony returned to Cleopatra, wrote:

> Then began this pestilent plague and mischief of Cleopatra's love (which had slept a long time, and seemed to have been utterly forgotten, and that Antonius had given place to better counsel).

Is Cleopatra ever forgotten by Shakespeare's Antony? In Egypt he believes that he must depart, 'Or lose myself in dotage' (I.2.118). The phrase is suggestive. Nobody recovers easily when they have come to the brink of losing themselves — and least of all when they fail to grasp the issues. In Rome, Antony's love for Cleopatra seems a time:

> . . . when poisoned hours had bound me up
> From mine own knowledge.
>
> (II.2.94–95)

'Poisoned' suggests an external influence. But a lover, however passive, helps to create the 'poison' of a relationship. Antony is naïve not only about self-knowledge — we may doubt if he ever had any to speak of — but also about his power to change. Instead of allowing time for growth, he tries a short cut. His marriage to Octavia seems to be an attempt at exorcism, a parody of mental growth in sensationalist redirection. Psychologically, it is too violent to succeed.

Shakespeare has changed Plutarch's account of a man returning to a former mistress into the story of an obsession. Apart from the brief vignette which opens the play, we see Antony and Cleopatra together only once before the decision to fight by sea in Act III scene 7. This is when Antony bids farewell to Cleopatra in Act I scene 3. She mounts a stupendous extravaganza. She pretends to swoon; Antony must stand further off; her love is 'riotous madness' — yet a second later we hear words of absolute lyricism:

> Eternity was in our lips and eyes,
> Bliss in our brows' bent; none our parts so poor
> But was a race of heaven.
>
> (I.3.35–37)

Then Antony is a liar whom she wants to punch. At last he gets in a word: Fulvia is dead. That stops her. But it only stops her for a moment. The performance starts again with a new element:

> Good now, play one scene
> Of excellent dissembling, and let it look
> Like perfect honour.

(I.3.78–79)

Antony is touchy about honour (see II.2.89, III.4.22–23) and Cleopatra must know this. He is aroused, 'You'll heat my blood; no more'. But Cleopatra presses on and on:

> CLEOPATRA You can do better yet; but this is meetly.
> ANTONY Now, by my sword —
> CLEOPATRA   And target. Still he mends.
>   But this is not the best. Look prithee, Charmian,
>   How this Herculean Roman does become
>   The carriage of his chafe.

(I.3.81–85)

She wants from him a theatricality to match her own. He will not rise. He cannot rise. So she satirises him to his face, flaunting how 'Herculean Roman' dwindles to 'chafe', a word of pets and temper, not rage.

Enobarbus later comments on Cleopatra's 'infinite variety' (II.2.241). We learn from I.3 that part of this variety is to arouse by attack where it hurts, and by a type of humiliation. She thrives on outrage and on pressing it to unthought of excess: the climax of Enobarbus's famous speech is:

> for vilest things
> Become themselves in her, that the holy priests
> Bless her when she is riggish.

(2.2.243–245)

'Vilest' is strong. Yet Cleopatra disarms sanctity even in this moment of dissoluteness.

The man who enters such a love may well become confused about priorities since dazzling reversals of priority are central to its energy and exhilaration — the eighteenth-century poet Alexander Pope, writing without reference to Cleopatra, articulates some of its paradoxes:

Yet ne'er so sure our passion to create,
As when she touch'd the brink of all we hate.

(*Epistle to a Lady*, ll.51–52)

What is also clear is that nobody easily breaks away from such a love. If they try a violent remedy, as Antony does, it is likely to go wrong. And if it goes wrong, the result will be collapse.

We see the collapse in the moment of tragedy, Antony's disastrous resolve to fight by sea. It is an absurd decision. Canidius and Enobarbus argue against it, the 'worthy soldier' pleads with his wounds against it. Antony has nothing to say for it. But Cleopatra has pronounced 'By sea; what else?' (III.7.28) and Antony merely repeats, 'By sea, by sea' (III.7.40) and 'I'll fight by sea' (III.7.48) as if taking part in a ritual. For this is in fact what he is doing. Cleopatra has declared her will. She is what matters. Fighting by sea is now a way of worshipping her. 'Away, my Thetis' (III.7.60) — she is a goddess of the ocean.

Shakespeare had always known the pity and pathos which comes from lingering over the final days of a ruined tragic hero. It was also part of his genius to create an extraordinary interplay of fantasy and fact in the consolations of his fallen men. We can see this in an early tragedy such as *Titus Andronicus*, and in *King Lear* which may have been written a year before *Antony and Cleopatra*.

Caesar knows that his rivals are doomed when Act IV opens, as does Cleopatra (IV.4.38). Shakespeare also tricks the audience by bringing forward the incident of Hercules abandoning Antony from after the land fight, where it occurs in Plutarch, to Act IV scene 3, *before* the fight. We admire Antony's spirit in going to fight but he too has little hope:

If fortune be not ours today, it is
Because we brave her.

(IV.4.4–5)

And Enobarbus abandons Antony (IV.5). But then, against all the odds and in a huge and thrilling reversal of expectation, Antony wins the battle:

CLEOPATRA   Lord of lords!
O infinite virtue, com'st thou smiling from
The world's great snare uncaught?

(IV.8.16–18)

This masterstroke of surprise has many effects. We know in our minds that the victory can only be temporary, but we exult in our hearts. Those we now love are alive. Losers win. Calculation and certainty are thwarted — and they are odious forces when negative. And suddenly the extravagance of Antony and Cleopatra is in a fresh focus. Earlier in the play, we marvelled at Enobarbus's account of Cleopatra's barge and we laughed at her wildness, sometimes with it, to an extent:

> He shall have every day a several greeting,
> Or I'll unpeople Egypt.
>
> (I.5.77–78)

But now the buoyancy of the lovers mirrors our own mood and we become at one with their high and revelling exhilaration:

> ANTONY   To this great fairy I'll commend thy acts,
> Make her thanks bless thee.
>   . . .
> CLEOPATRA   I'll give thee, friend,
> An armour all of gold; it was a king's.
> ANTONY   He has deserved it, were it carbuncled
> Like holy Phoebus' car
>
> (IV.8.12–29)

They sound like Oberon and Titania in their idioms of uninhibited and wild opulence.

Shakespeare's strategy is to establish this tone so that it can be exploited for at least two other purposes. The first is for the suicides. Antony and Cleopatra need to escape. But they alchemise this need into a rich vision of continuance which is as confident as the elemental immortality of the fairies in *A Midsummer Night's Dream*. Antony, a cloud which 'dislimns' (IV.14.10), invites Cleopatra:

> I come, my queen! — Eros! — Stay for me.
> Where souls do couch on flowers, we'll hand in hand,
> And with our sprightly port make the ghosts gaze:
> Dido and her Aeneas shall want troops,
> And all the haunt be ours. — Come, Eros, Eros!
>
> (IV.14.50–54)

Cleopatra joins the elements themselves: 'I am fire and air' (V.2.288).

The second use of this tone is more subtle though no less thrilling. There is a long stretch of the play between the 'false' victory of Act IV scene 8 and Cleopatra's suicide. Shakespeare's tactic is to use the complications of history in order to immerse us in what Cleopatra calls this 'dull world' (IV.15.61): accidents, miscalculations, failures of nerve, lies, manoeuvring, the daily treachery of administration — the Antoniad decamps, Antony bungles his suicide, Caesar botches his display of grief, Cleopatra juggles the invoices. It is dullness almost in the sense of Pope's satires.

Pope's ladies, too, are unpredictable. Are we confident of Cleopatra? Antony does not expect so robust a survivor to leave 'this dull world' even if she may say it is 'a sty' without him. She declares that she would like Caesar 'To give me conquered Egypt for my son' (V.2.19). She has kept vast sums of money back and her excuse is a survival plan in Rome (V.2.164–170). We cannot doubt that at least she toyed with these possibilities. But Cleopatra is also given by Shakespeare two explosions of supreme poetry, at IV.15.63–68 'The crown o'th'earth doth melt' and at more length, in V.2.76–100 where Cleopatra tells Dolabella her dream of Antony. The first passage is a gut reaction to Antony's death. The second is also provoked by a physical event, Cleopatra being 'surprised' by the Roman soldiers and disarmed by Proculeius. She is now a prisoner. But her response is to celebrate Antony in a speech which, like those of Oberon, is full of elemental and exultant metamorphoses:

> His legs bestrid the ocean; his reared arm
> Crested the world;
> ...
>
>   For his bounty,
> There was no winter in't; an Antony 'twas
> That grew the more by reaping.
>
> (V.2.82–88)

Do we doubt that she will commit suicide after this — even if she is also pushed to the brink by Caesar's threats about her children, icy for being so civil, and the prospect of humiliation in Rome?

Cleopatra's love, as we see it in Act I, demands intensity. It is the opposite of Octavia's 'still conversation' (II.6.121) which, to

Cleopatra, seems 'dull' (V.2.55). With Antony in the early scene, where she did not find intensity, she provoked it. When life forces its own intensity on her in the form of defeat, she rises to the occasion after their first failure at sea, and consoles Antony. Life suddenly matches her wishes by giving them an unexpected victory. But Antony is now dead and the lover of life can obtain life only on dull terms. So, she creates life in an intensity of imagined memory: Antony was Jove, a power of nature, a cornucopia of blessedness, an unquenchable source of gratification. '... t'imagine/ An Antony were nature's piece 'gainst fancy,/ Condemning shadows quite' (V.2.98–100). Yet nobody could sustain this act of imagining for long. The next step for Cleopatra is death. The alternative is a denial of her life force in a woman who lived for love.

Antony and Cleopatra sound at times like Oberon and Titania, yet because they are not immortal, they are both more noble and more comic than the fairies. Their fine poetry is a defiance of fate, and it is rich with self-discovery, not least of how much they mean to each other. Antony bungles his suicide, as he has bungled almost everything in the play. Cleopatra has a last flash of jealousy before reaching for the asp. The play ends not with the exhaustion of *King Lear* or *Macbeth* but with a warm if costly and anarchic triumph of love, of life so enriched by love that death is 'as a lover's pinch,/ Which hurts, and is desired' (V.2.294–295). The extremities of her goading of Antony in the first Act are now taken into herself, and they are used as an occasion for nobility. Yet, like her conversation with the Clown just before her suicide, the humour of these lines in their solemn context is tranquil and sublimely consoling.

AFTERTHOUGHTS

1

What significance does Gearin-Tosh attach in the first paragraph of this essay to Shakespeare's titling of *Antony and Cleopatra*?

2

Do you agree that it is doubtful that Antony 'ever' has any self-knowledge 'to speak of' (page 54)?

3

Do you agree with Gearin-Tosh's view of Antony's reasons for fighting by sea (page 56)?

4

Do you agree that we can measure the sincerity of any particular speech by its lyric intensity or 'supreme poetry' (page 58)?

Cedric Watts

Cedric Watts is Professor of English at Sussex University, and author of many scholarly publications.

ESSAY

Antony and Cleopatra: the moral and the ontological

In this title, the term 'moral' looks fairly easy but the term 'ontological' looks like trouble. It seems daunting and mysterious. 'Ontology' means 'discourse about being: the study of the very being or essential nature of things'. Think of a snail. I'm in my back garden and see a snail which has eaten one lettuce and is on its way to the next. 'What is that thing?', enquires a child nearby. 'A darned nuisance,' I reply; 'a garden pest.' And with that, I stamp on it. End of snail. Next day, I'm in the back garden and see another snail. This time I'm in a more philosophical mood. 'What is that thing?', enquires the child. 'A miracle of nature,' I reply. 'Look closely at it. See how it carries its house on its back. Observe its tiny sensitive horns. One touch with a blade of grass and the horns retract and the little head winces back into the shell. A marvel.' 'Indeed,' says the child. 'But if it's a miracle of nature, why did you stamp on one yesterday?' My exasperated answer is: 'Yesterday I was being moral, today I'm being ontological. Yesterday I was judging the snail by conventional moral criteria: in the garden, is this thing good or bad? Answer, bad. Today, on the other hand, I'm considering snailness: the distinctive nature of being a snail and not some other creature; its own peculiar kind of life...' (The child tiptoes away unnoticed at this point.) 'Notice that the ontological view often tends to question the moral view. It's harder to smash a snail once you've looked closely at its distinctive kind of life.'

I think it's the dramatisation of these two apparently contrasting outlooks, the moral and the ontological, that gives central thematic unity to Shakespeare's *Antony and Cleopatra*. As commentators often note, there are many patterns of contrasts in the play: Rome and Egypt; Octavia and Cleopatra; Octavius and Antony; duty and pleasure; war and love; the vulgar and the noble; the base and the majestic; failure and triumph; restraint and excess; water and fire; earth and air. It is, however, the apparent conflict between the moral and the ontological which can provide a basis for the most radical and most comprehensive scansion of the text. While soliciting judgements based on various orthodox ideas of good and bad, of the ethically sound and unsound, the play also solicits judgements based on the romantically subversive idea that what really matters is sheer magnificent intensity of being.

The contrast between the characters of Octavia and Cleopatra makes this point very clearly. If you judge them morally, using the criteria that would have been very traditional in Shakespeare's day and which are still familiar (if questionable) now, then Octavia wins. If a woman should be dutiful, truthful, chaste, conscientious and scrupulous, Octavia is much better than Cleopatra. If, however, you use the ontological criterion, fulness of being, then Cleopatra clearly wins; for Octavia, with her patient good will, her rather melancholy dutifulness and obedience, seems consistent but limited and unexciting. In Cleopatra there's that obvious, conspicuous range: she's true, false, seductive, spiteful, weak, strong, meek, arrogant, jealous, magnanimous, crafty, ingenuous, playful, grave. One kind of judgement leads to the other: it's the effort to make an orthodox moral judgement which leads us to see most clearly the ontological force. The more we say, 'This part of Cleopatra seems good, this part bad,' the more we test this aspect and that, the more the scales of judgement tend to collapse under the sheer weight of qualities that we're putting into the 'good' and 'bad' pans of the moral balance. The play seems to ask, finally, 'Which is better, a virtuous self or a full self? Should people be good, or should they be *vital*?' A vital personality may make orthodox moral judgements seem inadequate (because too schematic or selective); but the attempt to apply those familiar criteria may serve to reveal or emphasise such recalcitrant vitality.

If a teacher says to me, 'Is this poem good or bad?', that may be a direct question inviting a direct answer (e.g., 'I think it's good'); or it may be a tactical question designed to make me define and thus recognise fully the distinctive features of the poem. Shakespeare is a clever teacher: from the very start of *Antony and Cleopatra* he gets us involved in his tactical questions:

> Act I scene 1 [*Alexandria. A room in Cleopatra's palace*]
>
> *Enter Demetrius and Philo*
>
> PHILO   Nay, but this dotage of our general's
> O'erflows the measure. Those his goodly eyes,
> That o'er the files and musters of the war
> Have glowed like plated Mars, now bend, now turn
> The office and devotion of their view
> Upon a tawny front. His captain's heart,
> Which in the scuffles of great fights hath burst
> The buckles on his breast, reneges all temper,
> And is become the bellows and the fan
> To cool a gypsy's lust.
>
> *Flourish. Enter Antony, Cleopatra, her ladies Charmian and Iras, the train, with eunuchs fanning her*
>
> Look, where they come.
> Take but good note, and you shall see in him
> The triple pillar of the world transformed
> Into a strumpet's fool. Behold and see.
> CLEOPATRA   If it be love indeed, tell me how much.
> ANTONY   There's beggary in the love that can be reckoned.
> CLEOPATRA   I'll set a bourn how far to be beloved.
> ANTONY   Then must thou needs find out new heaven, new
> earth.
>
> *Enter a Messenger an Attendant*

MESSENGER   News, my good lord, from Rome.

ANTONY   Grates me! The sum.

(I.1.1–18)

Notice how the problem is posed in the very language as well as in the paraphrasable sense. Philo, the veteran campaigner, offers a soldier's view: once Antony was a great warrior, but now he's thrown himself away for a prostitute. The verse is powerfully energetic as it recalls the former Antony, whose eyes glowed like those of war-god Mars in battle, whose great heart could burst his breast-plate buckles in action, and who was the 'triple pillar of the world' (one of the triumvirate of Roman rulers — and, the phrasing suggest, one of three who, like Atlas, bore the very weight of the world). But now, it's alleged, this same Antony is slave to a swarthy face, is menial servant to a gipsy's lust, and is mere entertainer to a whore. The speech rings true as the expression of a soldier's disappointment in his leader; and we ask ourselves whether it is also true as a judgement of Antony; to answer that question we have to look hard and listen carefully to Antony and Cleopatra themselves. And immediately, as those two enter, a contrast is established. Philo had talked hyperbolically of the general and contemptuously of lust; but now Antony talks of love in romantic, hyperbolic terms. What Philo called a foolish infatuation, Antony depicts as a transcendent love which can't be measured by earthly standards. Philo thinks he's summed it up; Antony says it can't be summed up. Philo had complained of the reduction of the triple pillar of the world; Antony says that the known world and heaven itself won't suffice to define his love. Then, in the very moment when he's stressing transcendence — experience beyond earthly bounds — comes the ironic entry of the attendant bearing reminders of this world's demands and practicalities. And Antony says, 'Grates me! The sum' (something like the modern 'This grates! The gist?'). Just half a line after the lofty and rapturous 'Then must thou needs find out new heaven, new earth', that abruptly impatient 'Grates me! The sum'. We're being thrown to and fro not only between quite contrasting judgements but even between quite contrasting modes of speech. The oscillations are in the diction as well as in the claims.

Those oscillations are visual, too. At the beginning we saw a campaigner telling an acquaintance that Cleopatra was a mere brown gipsy and a whore; but then Cleopatra herself enters with Antony, her ladies and retinue, 'with eunuchs fanning her' — a whole procession. On stage it's a spectacular entry: it displays majesty, opulence, colour, beauty, the exotically oriental and the decadently luxurious, all at once. Visually, then, a stern moral judgement is brought into collision with a largely aesthetic judgement, and the claims of war and politics collide with the claims of romantic love. And just as we're adapting to the new claims and tones, in comes that attendant to say (in effect): love may orate but business calls. The extreme sense of richness in this play derives from the ways in which action, imagery and spectacle repeatedly establish patterns of mutually reinforcing contrasts: sweet against sour, luxury against hardihood, the lofty against the mundane, the vast against the petty, stillness against motion, the majestic against the sceptically realistic, the imaginative against the practical, the eternal against the temporal. The play makes our judgements swing and oscillate; the questions we're invited to pursue lead not to simple answers but to recognition of the richness of the whole dramatised wrangle. This is a drama of to-and-fro-ness, in location, imagery, plot and characterisation.

Quoting out of context seems more deceptive in the case of this play than in the case of many others. That's because there's a movement of irony around virtually every speech, however authoritative it may sound. In Act I scene 1, lines 33–40, Antony makes that great assertive outburst to Cleopatra which begins like this:

> Let Rome in Tiber melt, and the wide arch
> Of the ranged empire fall! Here is my space.
> Kingdoms are clay. Our dungy earth alike
> Feeds beast as man.

If you take it out of context, you may overlook the ironic way in which it's launched and closed. It's launched from Cleopatra's jibing, chiding, mocking, needling references to the power exerted over Antony by Octavius Caesar and 'shrill-tongued Fulvia': that's what starts the outburst, which ends with Antony embracing Cleopatra and saying:

> The nobleness of life
> Is to do thus — when such a mutual pair
> And such a twain can do't, in which I bind,
> On pain of punishment, the world to weet
> We stand up peerless.

When he declaims that, rising to a rhetorical climax of typically hyperbolic assertion, the response from Cleopatra is not 'We do indeed, and let the world take note!' It is:

> Excellent falsehood!
> Why did he marry Fulvia, and not love her?
> I'll seem the fool I am not.

Against commanding eloquence, shrewd sceptical mockery to goad and push him further. Octavius will prove to be astute in the politics of territorial conquest, but Cleopatra, from the start, is astute in the politics of amatory power.

Antony can be brave, magnanimous, generous, warm-hearted, adventurous, impulsive, affectionate; he is also shown to be brutal, jealous, cruel, foolhardy, fickle, and erratic in judgement. Cleopatra can be opulent, majestic, seductively erotic, shrewd, passionately sexual, brave and commanding. She can also be false, vain, bullying, petulant, selfish, capricious. Even her 'variety' is not 'infinite', for there are some tones and attitudes that lie outside her range. She obviously lacks the scrupulous moral dedication of a Cordelia or the wondering expectation of a Juliet. But she seems to approach as close to 'infinite variety' as any stage heroine can. One of the most astonishing passages comes in the last Act (V.2.219–221), when she reflects that if she's taken captive to Rome, this will happen:

> . . . I shall see
> Some squeaking Cleopatra boy my greatness
> I'th'posture of a whore.

She imagines that she'll have to watch some boy-actor play the part of Cleopatra the notorious courtesan. Of course, her words were originally spoken on the Jacobean stage not by an experienced actress of astonishing virtuosity but by a boy. That boy-actor who played Cleopatra must have been exceptionally talented; yet we don't even know his name. Shakespeare must have trusted totally his ability to perform convincingly the role of an experienced, intelligent, commanding and sexually voluptuous queen, otherwise the author would never have dared to include that bold reference to a squeaking boy-actor. He, and the lad in question, must have known they could get away with it. The imaginative wrench that occurs when we recall that Cleopatra was once 'a boy's part' tells us at once how persuasively rich and charismatic is her characterisation.

When Antony and Cleopatra prepare for death, Shakespeare could have made things easy for us by reducing complexity; by making us feel, 'Well, they may have had their faults, but they have at last become better, wiser, more virtuous; we can relax into conventional enjoyment of poignant tragic death-scenes.' To the last, however, intelligence keeps pace with the eloquence, and the oscillation between moral and ontological appraisals is maintained. Even there, as Antony and Cleopatra pass the supreme test of being ready (after all their past recriminations and deceptions) to die for each other and to elude humiliation, even there the complex realism is at work. Shakespeare could treat his literary sources very freely when he wished to. He could have departed from Plutarch's account of Antony's partly botched suicide; but he chose to preserve that botching. As in the source, too, we're shown Decretas deciding to present Antony's sword to Octavius as a way of ingratiating himself with a new master. Of course, when Antony has died, Cleopatra makes her superb tribute to him:

> For his bounty,
> There was no winter in't; an Antony it was
> That grew the more by reaping. His delights
> Were dolphin-like; they showed his back above
> The element they lived in.

After that poignant threnody, she asks:

> Think you there was or might be such a man
> As this I dreamt of?

And back comes the answer from Dolabella:

> Gentle madam, no.

(V.2.86–94)

This response doesn't cancel the tribute; doesn't erase it. But it does emphasise yet again the mutually critical disparity between, on the one side, the romantic excess of Antony and Cleopatra and, on the other, the familiar world; between their exalted self-dramatisations and the world of war, politics, ageing and change.

When Cleopatra prepares for her own death, with 'Give me my robe; put on my crown, I have/ Immortal longings in me' (V.2.279–280), even there the dominant sense of majesty is challenged. There's noble aspiration and dignity; but there's still some arrogance and vanity, a sense of conscious showmanship, a sense of an audience to be impressed. It's a deliberate performance. She's stage-managing her own death-scene, talking herself into belief in transcendence, and doing it magnificently. But life is not as tidy as stage-drama normally is, and Shakespeare knew it. When Cleopatra says, 'I am fire and air; my other elements/ I give to baser life', she has not quite abandoned a world which contains earth and water too. The way to fire and air is provided by the asp, the worm of Nilus's mud, the creature that leaves a slimy trail. She says:

> Peace, peace!
> Dost thou not see my baby at my breast,
> That sucks the nurse asleep?
>
> (V.2.307–309)

On stage, what we see, of course, is not nurse with baby at breast but queen with small snake at breast. Not new life but painless death. Even there, the disparity between her powerfully poignant metaphor and the immediate visual spectacle keeps judgement oscillating and feelings mixed. The oscillation is epitomised in Charmian's phrase 'A lass unparalleled': Cleopatra is unparalleled, yet she is a 'lass', which suggests one of many ordinary girls, perhaps country-girls; 'A lass' naturally sounds like 'Alas', which may suggest the price paid for such charismatic selfhood; and the phrase oddly echoes 'ass, unpolicied' — the phrase for Caesar who, though briefly thwarted, is still the global victor. At her death, Cleopatra is sumptuously dressed; she has donned her robe and crown; and Charmian says, 'golden Phoebus, never be beheld/ Of eyes again so royal!' (V.2.316–317). Yet the very next phrase is: 'Your crown's awry'. The tableau of majesty is imperfect after all. Cleopatra looks magnificent; but that crown is just slightly lopsided; the performance has been flawed, not as in conventional drama but as in life.

If we look back, we can see that throughout *Antony and Cleopatra* Shakespeare has set up a variety of orthodox ethical tests around the two central figures. There's the test of virtuous marital conduct. By that test, Octavia wins and Antony and Cleopatra lose. There's the test of political and military judgement. By that test, Octavius wins. There's the test of practical self-preserving common sense. There Decretas wins, and Antony and Cleopatra lose again. Then there's that test of powerful people which Shakespeare was very interested in applying: the test of magnanimity and generosity to social inferiors. Here there's a mixed answer. Antony can be hearty and companionable with his men, but he's capable of deserting them on the battle-field. He's generous enough to send Enobarbus's belongings to their owner when Enobarbus defects, but he's also capable of whipping a messenger. (Enobarbus's veering between admiration and criticism, loyalty to and defection from his master, is typical of the play's strategy.) Cleopatra, too, is affably familiar with some servants but bullying to others. The list could be greatly extended; but as it grows, we increasingly recognise that all such familiar criteria of judgement are in turn being called in question by the irreducible richness and intensity of the central relationship of the 'mutual pair'. Which is better, a virtuous life or an intense life? A successful career or a passionate career? Does rational judgement ever fully capture the distinctiveness of individuals? The play is largely about the sense that each of us holds more potential life than circumstances allow us to actualise. It demonstrates that without those resistances we would not fully recognise that potential. Recurrently, the play's imagery expresses a fierce questing for definition. Antony and Cleopatra try to define themselves and each other by reference to all the elements, to tides and dolphins, to season and fires, to kingdoms and empires, to sun, moon and stars. Antony is compared to Mars, Hercules and Bacchus; though he's also termed 'a strumpet's fool'. Cleopatra is called 'Egypt', yet she's the 'gipsy' too. Enobarbus says, 'We cannot call her winds and waters, sighs and tears', implying that perhaps we can; and this eastern queen can be termed a 'triple-turned whore' and 'a morsel, cold upon/ Dead Caesar's trencher', but yet 'thou day o' the world'. No comparison quite fits; no brief quotable definition sums up Antony and Cleopatra; but that ransacking for definition, that constant quest — *that* gets defined abundantly in the play. Here Shakespeare made superbly critical theatre about superbly theatrical lovers.

AFTERTHOUGHTS

1

What is Watts suggesting about Shakespeare's methods by describing him as 'a clever teacher' (page 63)?

2

What other speeches could you cite to support Watts's claim that 'there's a movement of irony around virtually every speech' (page 65)?

3

Compare Watts's view of Cleopatra's 'politics of amatory power' (page 66) with Flint's (pages 9–16).

4

What reason does Watts give for the 'fierce questing for definition' (page 69) within *Antony and Cleopatra?*

Peter Reynolds

Peter Reynolds is Lecturer in Drama at the Roehampton Institute of Higher Education, and author of Text into Performance *(Penguin, 1985).*

ESSAY

The divided self: the public and private lives of Antony and Cleopatra

A few years ago I recall watching on television the annual Remembrance Day parade from Whitehall, London. At the ceremony are present not only the Queen and members of her family, but also the leaders of all the main political parties. The main focus of the event comes when the Queen, the Prime Minister, and the leader of the opposition lay wreaths at the Cenotaph. On this occasion the leader of the opposition was Michael Foot. His appearance, or rather his clothes, were to cause a minor sensation the next day in the tabloid press. Almost everyone else present at the ceremony was dressed either in military uniform or in formal dress. David Steel, the then leader of the Liberal party, had on morning dress; the Prime Minister, Mrs Thatcher, wore a dark tailored suit, but Mr Foot, according to the tabloids, wore a 'donkey jacket'. In fact the coat he chose for the occasion was not as described, but the clothes he chose to appear in on this very public and formal occasion were, by comparison to those worn by other political figures, casual. He literally stood out from the rest, but in a way that he had neither anticipated nor intended. His underestimation of the existence of unwritten but powerful conventions governing the dress of public figures on occasions such as this brought him few friends and handed his political enemies free ammunition. Foot's failure sufficiently to take into account the importance of presenting an acceptable public image ultimately helped undermine his position as leader of a powerful political party, a party which, incidentally, under its present (1990) leadership, has demonstrated an acute awareness of the importance of the right public image.

In contemporary society, where television beams the images of prominent people into millions of living rooms simultaneously, and where those images are often carefully contrived by teams of public relations executives and advertising agencies, it is vital for any politician who wants to succeed in public life to be aware of the need, and to have the skills required, to construct and sustain an appropriate public persona. As the media have expanded in the twentieth century into the *mass* media, so the complaint amongst politicians that the successful marketing of individual personalities is probably the key to unlocking the ballot box rather than any serious promulgation of policies has become commonplace. But political life has always demanded that the personality of individual politicians is marketed as well as their policies.

The text of *Antony and Cleopatra* is littered with references clearly demonstrating that Shakespeare recognised the vital importance to political leaders of being able to present and sustain a positive, appropriate, and preferably charismatic public presence. The text also explores the difficulty of sustaining such an image, for the lives of Antony and Cleopatra are shown as a constant struggle between the conflicting demands of their public and private lives. In this essay I shall concentrate on the public image of four characters, all with immense political power, and all of whom recognise that the continued maintenance of their public reputations and images is crucial for their political survival: Pompey, Octavius Caesar, Mark Antony, and Cleopatra.

The threat posed to the regime of Octavius Caesar by the uprising of forces led by Pompey is real not simply because of any ability Pompey may have to command a viable military force, but because of the force of his public personality. In Act I scene 4 the messengers (representative of those without power) point out that Pompey's successful military campaign is being significantly aided by his apparent ability to attract to his cause the discontented followers of Caesar. These men have deserted Caesar because of his failure, or, if you prefer, the failure of his propaganda machinery, to win the battle for their hearts and minds:

> Pompey is strong at sea,
> And it appears he is beloved of those
> That only have feared Caesar

(I.4.36–38)

Pompey can inspire love ('The people love me' II.1.9), whereas Caesar loses it ('Caesar gets money where/ He loses hearts', II.1. 13–14). A messenger explains that Caesar has good reason to fear the power of Pompey: not his military might, but the effective propaganda surrounding him. It is the *name* of Pompey, his reputation, that is said to strike fear into the hearts of his enemies:

> No vessel can peep forth but 'tis as soon
> Taken as seen; for Pompey's name strikes more
> Than could his war resisted.

(I.4.53)

Caesar's apparent weakness as a military leader lies not in any lack of ability to raise a potentially viable military opposition to Pompey, but in his inability to command the right kind of public image. People do not appear to *love* him. Nonetheless, Shakespeare shows him to be a man with a highly developed and sophisticated political awareness. In Act III scene 4 he is angry that his sister Octavia, now married to Antony, has entered Rome without the ritual and ceremony appropriate to one of her rank:

> You come not
> Like Caesar's sister.
> . . .
> . . . you are come
> A market maid to Rome, and have prevented
> The ostentation of our love; which, left unshown,

Is often left unloved. We should have met you
By sea and land, supplying every stage
With an augmented greeting.

(III.6.42–55)

This failure to observe what we would now call protocol is not
only an opportunity lost for an appropriate public display, it
could also discredit Caesar by laying him open to charges of
neglecting his duty towards the wife of his valued ally — Mark
Antony — and thus of attempting to undermine Antony's public
position.

Octavius Caesar is presented then as a politician who understands the value of propaganda. He is also shown as a politician
who knows his own personal limitations but is able to take
appropriate measures to counter them. As he listens to the
messengers telling him of the threat posed by Pompey his
political brain is at work, and his immediate response to their
news is to summon to mind the main weapon in his counter
propaganda campaign: 'Antony . . .' (I.4.55). At the beginning of
this scene Caesar had been castigating the private behaviour of
Antony as 'womanly', but now he needs not simply the man, but,
far more importantly, the myth of the heroic superman he
represents. That mythical power of Antony, his public reputation
as an invincible hero, is what is required to turn the tide in the
war of personalities. Caesar's rhetorical skill now begins to
create a classic piece of myth-making propaganda. He recon-
structs an image that at the beginning of the scene he had been
keen to belittle. We hear now not of the 'man who is the abstract
of all faults/ That all men follow' (I.4.9–10) but of the fabulous
heroic figure who:

> . . . didst drink
> The stale of horses and the gilded puddle
> Which beasts would cough at. Thy palate then did deign
> The roughest berry, on the rudest hedge.
> Yes, like the stag when snow the pasture sheets,
> The barks of trees thou browsèd'st. On the Alps
> It is reported thou didst eat strange flesh,
> Which some did die to look on. And all this —
> It wounds thine honour that I speak it now —

Was borne so like a soldier, that thy cheek
So much as lanked not.

(I.4.61–71)

The rhetorical conjuring of the myth of Mark Antony the super-hero comes about in this case because Caesar recognises the pressing need to re-invent it. The people may not love Caesar, but they do love, and therefore will follow into battle, Mark Antony.

In the play, Mark Antony is continually shown as being very aware of his own image and how important it is to him to sustain it. In an interesting scene late in the play (IV.2), Shakespeare demonstrates how manipulative Antony is in order to sustain his special identity and retain the loyalty of his followers. In this scene Cleopatra watches with some astonishment how Antony flatters his servants in order to reinforce their loyalty. Enobarbus recognises that this is not the face of sincerity, but that it is contrived, Antony is acting, using an old technique: 'one of those odd tricks which sorrow shoots/ Out of the mind' (lines 14–15), carefully contrived 'To make his followers weep' (line 24). Later in Act IV we are shown Antony about to play another but much more central role on a bigger stage than that of a kind and modest master. Occasion demands that he must become what his public (and Caesar) expect of him: the heroic man of war. In scene 4 Antony prepares to be seen on the public stage and puts on an appropriate costume: he is to play his part in armour. Shakespeare actually shows this transformation from the private man into the public figure. It is a scene the importance of which is easily underestimated when reading the play as opposed to seeing it enacted, for in performance what the arming can demonstrate is the literal as well as the symbolic transformation of the man into the mythical hero eulogised by Octavius Caesar. Unlike Mr Foot at the Cenotaph, Mark Antony shows a consummate mastery of *all* the arts of self-presentation.

The transformation of Antony is given added force in this scene by being effected in part by the efforts of another mythical figure whose legend is equal, if very different in kind, to his: Cleopatra. She becomes his servant. Even though Cleopatra's power is not that of a charismatic military leader (indeed she is shown not to be intimate with the rituals of military life and fumbles the buckling on of Antony's armour), she nonetheless exercises considerable power. At times during the play, that power threatens to undermine and subvert the codes of honour that underpin Roman society. The alleged sybaritic delights of her court ('I'th'East my pleasure lies', II.3.41) and her female sexuality are seen as powerful because of her legendary ability to charm and seduce great men. As well as Antony, Julius Caesar has been her lover, and by subjecting them to her will she threatens to make them neglect their public duty to the State in pursuit of private pleasure. This is the line of argument articulated by the two Roman soldiers, Demetrius and Philo, whose commentary on life in Egypt begins the play. From the beginning of the action we learn of those who are greatly concerned by the private behaviour of a public figure. They speak of their general's 'dotage' and of how his heroic masculine self (i.e. the public man) has been overcome by a 'gypsy's lust'.

The image of Cleopatra created in part by Roman militaristic society (and recognised and sustained by her because she understands its worth in political terms) is the embodiment of a very different kind of world to that of Rome. Cleopatra's Egypt represents a world of pleasure and sensuous fulfilment, a world to be tolerated and even envied just as long as the pursuit of pleasure does not lead away from the path of duty to the State. The classic evocation of all that Egypt and its queen represent comes from Enobarbus. In Act II scene 2 he tells an eager audience of soldiers, noses metaphorically pressed up against a shop window, of the contents of this distant and mysterious world:

> MAECENAS Eight wild boars roasted whole at a breakfast, and but twelve persons there. Is this true?
> ENOBARBUS This was but as a fly by an eagle. We had much more monstrous matter of feast...
>
> (II.2.184–187)

Of course this has all the hallmarks of exaggeration; it is part of the process of myth-making in which travellers returning from rare and exotic locations often indulge. Enobarbus is rather like a person who wins a competition in which the first prize is a holiday in a faraway tropical 'paradise'. When he gets there he finds not exactly paradise, but an island that is humid, even hostile, and with very little to do all day except count the days to the date of his return. But he can't of course bring himself to tell the entire truth about a place that he has been dreaming about for years, so he writes postcards home extolling its 'rare beauty' and creating fictions, stories of the marvellous things he has experienced in his distant exile. Although I am not suggesting that Enobarbus is lying, he does deliver a wonderfully evocative verbal postcard in the famous description he gives of Cleopatra's progress down the river Nile. This is surely a fine example of how myths are constructed and *why*. On the one hand Cleopatra recognises the need to construct an image that will emphasise her difference from everyday experience, and on the other Enobarbus demonstrates the eagerness with which such fictions are consumed:

> ENOBARBUS   The barge she sat in, like a burnished throne,
>   Burned on the water. The poop was beaten gold;
>   Purple the sails, and so perfumèd that
>   The winds were love-sick with them. The oars were silver,
>   Which to the tune of flutes kept stroke and made
>   The water which they beat to follow faster,
>   As amorous of their strokes. For her own person,
>   It beggared all description. She did lie
>   In her pavilion, cloth-of-gold of tissue,
>   O'erpicturing that Venus where we see
>   The fancy outwork nature. On each side her
>   Stood pretty dimpled boys, like smiling cupids,
>   With divers-coloured fans, whose wind did seem
>   To glow the delicate cheeks which they did cool,
>   And what they undid did.
> AGRIPPA   O, rare for Antony!

(II.2.196–211)

Those listening to Enobarbus cannot of course test the literal truth of what he says. It has rather a poetic truth in that it succeeds in arousing a series of seductive images in the mind's eye of the listener. They consume the poetry and the rhetoric of fiction and doubtless go on to retell and elaborate still further this small fragment of the public image of the Queen of Egypt.

It would seem in the last Act that Octavius Caesar, that cool political thinker, will succeed in turning the myth of Cleopatra to his own advantage. He has defeated Mark Antony, and at the end of the play threatens to expose Cleopatra to humiliation in Rome:

> CLEOPATRA Know you what Caesar means to do with me?
> DOLABELLA I am loath to tell you what I would you knew.
> CLEOPATRA Nay, pray you, sir.
> DOLABELLA   Though he be honourable —
> CLEOPATRA He'll lead me, then, in triumph?
> DOLABELLA Madam, he will. I know't.
>
> (V.2 106–110)

Such is the power of the image of Cleopatra that when Caesar finally meets the mythical queen face to face, and for the first time, the text indicates that he has trouble in recognising her: 'Which is the Queen of Egypt?' (V.2 112). And Cleopatra herself has to be told who it is asking the question: 'It is the Emperor, madam' (line 113). Cleopatra looks, Caesar discovers, not like a goddess, but a woman indistinguishable from other women. Once Caesar sees for himself what Cleopatra already knows — the reality behind the carefully contrived public mask, 'No more but e'en a woman' (IV.15.72) — then he astutely recognises the potential propaganda value to him of displaying her in Rome not in a gilded barge, but pulled along humiliatingly behind his chariot. Not only has Caesar one eye on cementing his victory by exposing the myth of Cleopatra (he has already destroyed that of Antony by defeating him in battle), he has the other on the construction of his own mythology: 'her life in Rome/ Would be *eternal* in our triumph' (V.1 65–66 — my italics).

It is Cleopatra's recognition of how Caesar intends to make political capital out of her by building up his own image at the expense of hers (V.2.106–110) that drives her to the action which, although it proves her mortality, is intended by her to preserve for ever her mythical status. It is being exposed to the everyday vulgarity of the lives of ordinary people, being parodied, and the consequent loss of her mythical status, that Cleopatra fears:

> CLEOPATRA   Now, Iras, what think'st thou?
>   Thou, an Egyptian puppet, shall be shown
>   In Rome as well as I. Mechanic slaves

> With greasy aprons, rules, and hammers shall
> Uplift us to the view. In their thick breaths,
> Rank of gross diet, shall we be enclouded,
> And forced to drink their vapour.
> IRAS   The gods forbid!
> CLEOPATRA   Nay, 'tis most certain, Iras. Saucy lictors
> Will catch at us like strumpets, and scald rhymers
> Ballad us out o'tune. The quick comedians
> Extemporally will stage us, and present
> Our Alexandrian revels. Antony
> Shall be brought drunken forth, and I shall see
> Some squeaking Cleopatra boy my greatness
> I'th'posture of a whore.

(V.2 207–221)

Thus what Antony had previously called 'Our slippery people' (I.2.186) are portrayed in Cleopatra's imagination as very ready to mock, belittle, and reduce a hero to a drunkard, and a fabled queen to a whore. Of course, what the play has shown to its audience is neither a drunkard nor a whore, but neither have they seen mythical larger-than-life figures. They have *heard* of such people (from Caesar and Enobarbus), but the reality they have witnessed is different. Audiences are continually confronted with the gap between what the language of speeches like those of Caesar and Enobarbus conjure in the mind's eye, and the reality actually before it — a man and a woman with legendary reputations making a series of tragic blunders that emphasise not their difference from the rest of humanity, but their human frailty. What Antony actually does flies in the face of everything his public image is meant to embody. As an almost unbelieving soldier says after Antony's first flight from the confrontation with Caesar:

> I never saw an action of such shame.
> Experience, manhood, honour, ne'er before
> Did violate so itself.

(III.10.21–23)

Enobarbus cannot actually bring himself to look at the reality of what his master has done: 'Mine eyes did sicken at the sight, and could not/ Endure a further view' (III.10.16–17).

The actions of both Antony and Cleopatra in the last two Acts of the play continually threaten to expose and destroy the mythology surrounding them. Yet, despite the great soldier fleeing from battle in humiliation, his attempt at a heroic ending becoming a bungled suicide, the depiction of the legendary queen as weak, fickle and a coward, and the cruel spectacle of black comedy when the half-dead 'old lion' is heaved up by women into the monument, the play does not end in the destruction of the mythical lovers, but with their resurrection.

In the last scene, when Cleopatra realises what Caesar intends to make of the defeat of Antony and the capture of herself, she begins to re-fashion the public image of Mark Antony: 'there was an emperor Antony' (line 76):

> CLEOPATRA His legs bestrid the ocean; his reared arm
> Crested the world; his voice was propertied
> As all the tunèd spheres, and that to friends;
> But when he meant to quail and shake the orb,
> He was as rattling thunder. For his bounty,
> There was no winter in't: an Antony it was
> That grew the more by reaping. His delights
> Were dolphin-like; they showed his back above
> The elements they lived in. In his livery
> Walked crowns and crownets; realms and islands were
> As plates dropped from his pocket.
> DOLABELLA   Cleopatra —
> CLEOPATRA Think you there was or might be such a man
> As this I dreamt of?
> DOLABELLA   Gentle madam, no.
> CLEOPATRA You lie . . .
>
>   (V.2.82–95)

Finally, after fashioning the final monumental image of Antony, she turns to the image of herself. For the first and last time, the audience are to see her as the familiar icon. She summons her women to dress her in her 'best attires', just as, previously, she had helped to dress Antony. Her task now is to play a part that will transcend reality. The stage directions indicate the return of Charmian and Iras with 'a robe, crown, and other jewels', and with these properties the final regal picture is composed:

> Give me my robe; put on my crown; I have
> Immortal longings in me.

(V.2 279–280)

The audience are left knowing that the image is false, having seen why and how it was created, but satisfied nonetheless. They know about the divided selves — the public and private faces of great men like Caesar, Antony, and that of the fabled queen herself, but what is lasting about Antony and Cleopatra, like Dido and Aeneas, or Romeo and Juliet, is not the reality that surrounded them, but the mythology.

AFTERTHOUGHTS

How helpful (and/or fair on Michael Foot!) do you find the anecdote which opens this essay?

2

Compare Reynolds's interpretation of the reasons behind Caesar's praise of Antony (pages 75–76) with Cunningham's (page 109).

3

Do you agree that Antony 'shows a consummate mastery of *all* the arts of self-presentation' (page 76)?

4

Is Cleopatra's public image at the end of the play entirely 'false' (page 82)?

Charles Moseley
Charles Moseley teaches English at Cambridge University and at the Leys School, Cambridge. He is the author of numerous critical studies.

ESSAY

Speaking pictures: visual symbol in *Antony and Cleopatra*

It is perhaps inevitable that most of us spend far more time reading Renaissance plays than watching them. We are, quite rightly, very ready to give the verbal text a great deal of analytical attention, yet as we do so it is all too easy to forget that theatre is a visual as well as a verbal art. Renaissance plays are not books, but a visual and auditory experience played in a special building on a stage that carried a great deal of symbolic charge for their audiences. The actors, like the authors and producers, were as ready to exploit the resources of gesture and visual symbol as an important and precise means of communication as audiences were to expect them.[1]

Many critics of the time repeated the cliché that a poem was a 'speaking picture', and a picture a 'silent poem'; there is a clear

---

[1] This point is discussed in much more detail in the early chapters of my *Shakespeare's History Plays: 'Richard II' to 'Henry V': The Making of a King* (Harmondsworth, 1988).

expectation of the interchangeability of the sign systems of the two arts, and a play is, of course, a special sort of poem. To look at a Renaissance play as a picture suddenly freed into movement and sound can be extremely fruitful: not only will the terms of contemporary art criticism be relevant to its general discussion, but also the symbols encountered in the visual arts may very well offer a way of looking at the detail of what is said and done on stage that will deeply affect our understanding of the play as a whole.

Of course, at this distance of time there are many things that are unknowable both about how things were played on stage — after all, in Shakespeare's case he was there to tell the actors how he wanted things done, and the actors could (and probably did) argue with him — and about the precise way in which ideas communicated visually might be received by an audience. But there is at least one source that allows us to make a good number of intelligent inferences. Emblem books were published in vast numbers in the latter part of the sixteenth century and throughout the seventeenth. Their concern is almost exclusively moral; their method is to combine a symbolic picture, often drawn from a classical story or from natural history, with a witty summarising motto and a brief verse exploring the subtleties of the picture. They can be shown to have had a huge importance: the core of symbolic visual reference they grew out of (and in turn reinforced) in men's minds affected not only the detail and the composition of full-scale paintings and statues, but also the imagery of poetry, the decoration of rooms and buildings, the way people of rank dressed, and even the serving of food and the making of table decorations. If we remember that pictures were the usual Renaissance way of conceptualising abstractions — like Prudence, or Fortitude, or Fortune, or Time — it should not be too surprising to find references to ideas visually conceived profuse in the discourse of Renaissance drama.[2] Recognising them can demand that we seriously alter the way we have been accustomed to read a play;

---

[2] The development of the emblem and its importance for this issue is examined in my *A Century of Emblems, curiously culled and delightfully displayed: an introductory anthology* (London, 1989).

indeed, visual reference and visual appearance may constitute a level of irony to which the verbal text alone gives us little clue.

Space forbids an examination of all the visual symbols in *Antony and Cleopatra*. Here I shall concentrate on three, one referred to in the imagery, one implied by the structure, and one seen on stage: Antony's being likened to a Colossus, the peculiar organisation of the earlier scenes of the play, and the way Cleopatra's death is staged.

> His legs bestrid the ocean; his reared arm
> Crested the world; his voice was propertied
> As all the tunèd spheres, and that to friends;
> But when he meant to quail and shake the orb,
> He was as rattling thunder. For his bounty,
> There was no winter in't; an Antony it was
> That grew the more by reaping. His delights
> Were dolphin-like; they showed his back above
> The element they lived in. In his livery
> Walked crowns and crownets; realms and islands were
> As plates dropped from his pocket.
>
> (V.2.82–92)

Here of course we are not dealing with something seen, but something we are to imagine; we are given a lot of help to do so visually. The Colossus-image is common enough — it is applied to Julius Caesar, for example (*Julius Caesar* I.2.135ff) — and its ancestry is obviously the statue of Apollo, god of Wisdom, that once stood at the entrance to the harbour at Rhodes. The visual dimension in the passage is detailed and consistent: an Antony showing kingly, even godlike, authority and largesse, of huge size, bestriding the world, his arm like a heraldic crest. Briefly, we picture an emperor in procession before returning to the idea of huge bodily size. Now in several emblem books of earlier and later date the Colossus appears: for example, in George Wither's *A Collection of Emblemes* (London, 1635), which used the engravings of Rollenhagen's *Nucleus Emblematum Selectissimorum* (Utrecht, 1611), there are two such emblems, and both of them are associated with that quality about which Renaissance moral and political philosophers were much exercised, namely Wisdom. Wither is merely usual in so doing, and even if he were not, his attachment of that quality to the symbol of the Colossus would give us a line on how an audience might have received the image of this passage.

In the first of his illustrations (I. xxxi) a figure wearing a kingly crown stands on a globe with the signs of the zodiac marked on its ecliptic. He holds a sceptre, and a book on which divine light is showered, and on his breast is engraved an open eye, symbolising understanding and knowledge. The motto is 'Hee, over all the Starres doth raigne,/ That unto Wisdome can attaine'. The subject of the emblem is a personal wisdom, allowing the wise man to be moral master of the influences of the tuned spheres and the visiting moon. (Cleopatra's new-found purpose, incidentally, allows her to reject the Isis/moon she has been linked with throughout: 'now the fleeting moon/ No planet is of mine' V.2.240–241). The wise man is above Fortune. In Wither's second emblem (III.xxix), the Colossus stands on a globe, wearing an imperial crown, and holds in one hand an open book of Law and in the other the sword of Justice, flourished in a heraldic gesture reminiscent of so many crests. Behind him are scenes of good government, of commerce and of the administration of justice. The motto 'When Law, and Armes, together meet,/ The World descends, to kisse their feet' stresses that here the virtue is political wisdom, the conjunction of law and power in the equity that is an important quality of the Good Prince. And, interestingly, Wither suggests that when they are conjoined, universal empire of the three parts of the world follows. It would certainly seem, therefore, that the Colossus-image in *Antony and Cleopatra* is not just part of the 'apocalyptic', 'grand', 'divine', imagery so characteristic of the play and so closely linked to its two heroes, but actually modifies and deepens a contemporary audience's understanding of the specific moral context of Antony's character and action and — more importantly, perhaps — Cleopatra's understanding of it. Antony as a ruler and as a dramatic hero has at some point to be evaluated against the ideals Renaissance men held of the Good Prince; and the Colossus-image points us in that direction, and in so doing raises questions about Antony that are central to the play.

But there is no sense in which wisdom can automatically be linked with the two heroes; rather, they seem to exemplify its opposite. Yet I am sure that a large part of the play's discussion does focus on the nature of true wisdom and true prudence, and the Colossus-image in fact focuses in our minds a set of ideas associated with Antony which have been very apparent in the structure and language of the play. The rapid and contrasting alternation, especially of the early scenes, across half a world between Rome and Egypt, with Antony, or the discussion of Antony, as the only link between them, is a device Shakespeare uses nowhere else and, I suggest, is a daring way of illuminating the moral dilemma of Antony. To see why, we have to consider the explicit and at first sight functionless linking of Antony with Hercules which is stressed several times in the play. The music heard under the stage as Hercules deserts Antony is meaningless to a modern audience, but we may be sure it was not to the original one. Further, Antony believes he has been deserted by Cleopatra as Hercules was by Deianira (IV.12.43); again, the audience knew their mythology, and we may be sure they saw more point here than mere self-pitying grandiose comparison.

A favourite Renaissance story, which is the subject of many paintings — for example by Raphael — is the Choice of Hercules. Hercules, so the story goes, was approached by two women, the one, hideous and deformed behind her beautiful mask, offering him sensual pleasure, the other offering power with work and responsibility. What fascinated the humanists about this story (which originates with Xenophon) was not so much the moral choice (though that certainly did) as the possibility of reconciling pleasure and virtue by a higher wisdom than that which would make the obvious and immediate choice. Traditionally, Hercules's descent into Hades was supposed to have taught him virtues of courage, the rejection of avarice and the mastery and proper use of pleasure — issues not at all far away from the tragedy of Antony. Proper fortitude is one of its concerns; the rejection of avaricious rule is stressed — not least in the passage discussed on page 86 and the generosity that breaks Enobarbus's heart — and the mastery (or not) of pleasure is the eastern rock on which the ship of state founders (or so it seems). After his ordeals, Hercules achieves a blessedness sealed by his ascent to Olympus; Antony's crisis culminates with him being lifted up into a symbol of durability and fame, a pyramid. Furthermore, the Egyptian scenes are dominated by Cleopatra (linked with Isis and Venus) in whose palace Antony has an attendant called Eros, who arms Antony, as in many Renaissance paintings

Venus arms, and disarms, Mars. Against her strong verbal and visual presence is set the virtuous Octavia, who seeks concord between her husband and her brother, and who is made to contrast in every possible way with Cleopatra — verse, described looks, values, foresight. Antony is quite conscious of the differing sets of values of each locale, recognising that 'I'th'East my pleasure lies' while equally acknowledging 'I have not kept my square'.

Here again visual treatments of the Hercules theme give us clues about how the Hercules references, and the structural opposition of the scenes, might have been received, and perhaps gave Shakespeare a clue for their stage treatment. Two emblems are good examples. In Geffrey Whitney's *A Choice of Emblemes* (Leyden, 1586) Hercules is shown hesitating between Venus — Love — and Minerva — Power with Wisdom. Behind the figures is a scene virtually identical to the 'tragic' stage set described by Sebastiano Serlio in *Achitettura* (Venice, 1551), with in the background a circular temple symbolic of the 'concord of this discord'. This emblem picture, encapsulating as it does the Renaissance understanding and moralisation of the Choice of Hercules, suggests both that the best way to discuss the choice itself is by the sort of bi-polar structure Shakespeare has adopted, and that we ought to look much more deeply than that initial opposition for the heart of the play's meaning.

In Wither's emblem on this theme, I.xxii, the ideas implicit in Whitney's are extended and made more open. The re-used picture shows physical beauty as a mere mask; death is the end of that road, and the gathered rosebuds wither in their urn while Virtue's plant grows straight and tall. Virtue has not only a book, but a caduceus twined with the serpents of wisdom. Hercules is shown at the moment of hesitation between them.

Antony/Hercules's career in the play turns on exactly that hesitation and final choice. But if Hercules found a way through suffering to reconcile Pleasure and Virtue, some such movement might be expected in a dramatic Antony. As we have seen, the overtones of Cleopatra's Colossus-image suggest such a wisdom was attained, though at the cost of loss of the world and of worldly power; and it is a fact that there is no watcher of the play who does not feel more inclined to go into the dark with Antony and Cleopatra than stay around with the 'ass unpolicied',

Caesar, conventionally wise and prudent as he may be. Perhaps, indeed, the play is asserting that there is a wisdom which transcends what we normally call wisdom, a prudence that sees far enough to recognise the shallowness of the values we normally associate with that concept. And here the presentation of the death of Cleopatra is crucial.

In V.2.279ff, Cleopatra is magnificently dressed and crowned as a queen. The elaborateness of Jacobean stage props and clothes is well known, and quite apart from the verse, this part of the scene would be stunning. Her royalty is quite unambiguously stressed by action, vision, and by Charmian's last words: 'It is well done, and fitting for a princess/ Descended of so many royal kings' (lines 325–326). But there is more going on than mere magnificence. Everybody knew that Cleopatra uses an asp to kill herself, but the visual effect of seeing a royal queen holding a snake draws in a complex of quite different ideas.

Snakes, whatever their other less attractive characteristics, have always been associated with subtlety, wisdom and knowledge. They are also associated with prudence, and it is this, and the linking of that prudence with royalty, that is crucial to this moment. The association of snakes with prudence is easy to demonstrate. For example, the painting of the Seven Virtues by Pesellino (now in the Birmingham Museum of Art in Birmingham, Alabama) has Prudence as a queen, holding the mirror that is another of her attributes, holding a serpent to her breast. Cesare Ripa, whose encyclopaedia of myth and visual symbol had a huge influence throughout Europe from the end of the sixteenth century, describes Prudence as a lady holding a serpent on her arm. Wither (II.xlvii; III. xvii) takes the association for granted. In fact the snake is an inseparable attribute of Prudence and is on its own a frequent symbol of wisdom. It is also frequently associated with royalty — Catherine de Medici's device, for example, was a star surmounted by a crowned serpent biting its tail, with a motto that claimed that prudence was more powerful than fate, and the Hatfield House portrait of Elizabeth I has the snake of Prudence on her left sleeve.

This severely modifies a modern reading of the scene. The visual pun of Prudence/Queen is inescapable, and the association, as I have demonstrated, of the serpent's wisdom with self-rule and political rule is also involved. Moreover, in the Pesellino painting the type of the prudent ruler, Solon, is at Prudence's feet; at Cleopatra's metaphorical feet, rejected by her as 'ass unpolicied', is Caesar, the representative of Roman rule and law. By her death Cleopatra cheats him of his policy's triumph over her (apparent) conventional unwisdom. But, just as we ask what sort of wisdom it is that Antony might have won, so we must ask what sort of prudence it could possibly be that Cleopatra shows.

The opening words of the play state unambiguously the Roman view of Antony's moral stance, and, by implication, of the values Cleopatra represents: 'dotage'. Yet the play opens up a discussion of that conduct, through the Choice of Hercules, through the ideas of wisdom, to the point where we see that the issues are not so simple. At key points in the play both heroes are given crucial visual referents which make us see the immediate human action as typifying something universal, general, cosmic, where the values may well not be so obvious — Antony as the Colossus, and the key, climactic icon of Cleopatra as Prudence. This latter is not simply heavily ironic, confirming the dismissive valuation of Philo — it is far too emotionally powerful and convincing for that. Taken as the culmination of a chain of references exemplified verbally, conceptually, and structurally, it necessarily calls in question the usual values and the customary antitheses between Virtue and Pleasure. What on the one hand may appear as a moral and indeed political evil may acquire a different force when the human actors are seen as symbols of cosmic principles, as the imagery so often makes us do. The final icon suggests that there is a higher wisdom, a higher prudence, a concord of this discord, for lack of which the conventional ideas of empire are the poorer. Antony's being hoisted aloft, and Cleopatra's immortal longings, suggest they have found a paradoxical wisdom that is no plant that grows on mortal soil.

AFTERTHOUGHTS

1

What reasons does Moseley give at the beginning of this essay for considering a Renaissance play 'as a picture suddenly freed into movement and sound' (page 85)?

2

Explain the relevance to Moseley's argument of his account of the two pictures of the Colossus in George Wither's *A Collection of Emblemes* (pages 86–87).

3

Can we be sure that the original audiences of Shakespeare's plays 'knew their mythology' (page 88)?

4

How convincing do you find Moseley's interpretation of the snake symbol (page 90)? Does this modify your view of the play's ending in any way?

Mark Spencer Ellis

*Mark Spencer Ellis is Head of English
at Forest School and a Chief Examiner
in English A level for the London
Examinations Board.*

ESSAY

A cloud that's dragonish

> 'How can you let them speak to you like that?' Elena said to her
> husband. 'Will you allow them to speak to an academician in
> such a way?'

The extract from today's *Times* (27 December 1989) is both
shocking and pathetic. Nicolae Ceausescu and his wife Elena
were within minutes of being shot. The former president of
Romania was being tried by the court which he must have
known was about to sentence them both to death. Elena's
remarks, quoted above, are the only things she said, according to
the Reuter report. What dignity, what status, what sense of
identity is suggested by 'academician'? A title which implies
deserved honour but one which every reader of the report will
recognise as a self-creation, an 'honour' as transparent as those
which the pigs award themselves in *Animal Farm*. Elena
Ceausescu's outburst is shocking because we know what happened next; it is pathetic because she clings to a title which no
one else acknowledges as having any validity. We are reluctant
to say 'how absurd' because death, in particular death by firing
squad, isn't absurd. We know that logic doesn't allow subsequent
events to confer dignity on what is absurd, but then we are
uneasily aware that the whole idea of things being innately
absurd or tragic doesn't stand up to close examination. Yet the
tone of the report is unsure: 'He occasionally touched his wife's

hands which were folded in her lap. Her face betrayed no emotion.' Why the second sentence? The report is searching for moments of humanity and dignity which help us to come to terms with death.

> The miserable change now at my end
> Lament nor sorrow at, but please your thoughts
> In feeding them with those my former fortunes,
> Wherein I lived; the greatest prince o'th'world,
> The noblest

> (IV.15.51–55)

This is not an exact parallel though many of the same comments do still apply. However, an audience does not necessarily respond in the same way as the reader of a newspaper. In particular, Antony's clinging to his titles as a source of comfort to himself and Cleopatra is something we are more prepared to allow him than we are to find 'academician' a valid label for the Ceausescus. What grounds are there for seeing Antony as 'the greatest prince o'th'world', and what are the social forces which make him so eminent?

The political world of *Antony and Cleopatra* is a violent one. While the text allows us to see conflicts in terms of character (and generations of examiners have cheerfully reduced the play to high-grade soap opera through questions implying that it is merely a series of personality clashes), we are always aware that conflicts have a price. When Caesar addresses Pompey the acknowledged alternative to a truce is wholesale killing:

> ... let us know
> If 'twill tie up thy discontented sword
> And carry back to Sicily much tall youth
> That else must perish here.

> (II.6.5–8)

Death is the currency of political negotiations. Caesar's offer to Cleopatra after Actium is straightforward — safety: 'so she/ From Egypt drive her all-disgracèd friend/ Or take his life there' (III.12.21–23). The card he plays to prevent Cleopatra from committing suicide is to threaten her children:

> ... you shall bereave yourself
> Of my good purposes, and put your children

To that destruction which I'll guard them from
If thereon you rely.

(V.2.130–133)

It is Caesar who points us to what came before Cleopatra's death: 'She hath pursued conclusions infinite/ Of easy ways to die' (V.2.353–354). When she identifies the asp as the 'pretty worm of Nilus there,/ That kills and pains not' (V.2.243–244), her confidence is based on the 'infinite' experiments she has carried out in watching condemned men die, in order to find the method which best suits her.

When we are presented with real violence — the humiliated whipped Thidias in III.13 or, more important, the corpse of Pacorus in III.1 — the moments are central in revealing the forces which give characters their political definition. Antony orders the whipping in order to reassert his sense of status: 'I am/ Antony yet' (III.13.92–93). The effect is shocking and pathetic, and the shock comes from our imaginative perception of real pain for Thidias. The physical agony of others is the currency of the leading characters:

> . . . tell him he has
> Hipparchus, my enfranchèd bondman, whom
> He may at pleasure whip, or hang, or torture,
> As he shall like, to quit me.

(III.13.148–151)

The discussion between Ventidius and Silius in III.1 is a clinical dissection of power politics. In particular, the former's measured speech (lines 11–27) would not be out of place in private and leisured surroundings. The point is that it is on a battlefield, centre stage is a corpse. It is obvious how Pacorus met his death, and he is now due to be paraded 'Before our army' (line 4). Ventidius is well aware that 'Caesar and Antony have ever won/ More in their officer than person' (lines 16–17), and the reassuring message that Antony will receive is simply a political necessity for Ventidius's own career prospects:

> I'll humbly signify what in his name,
> That magical word of war, we have effected;
> How, with his banners and his well-paid ranks,

The ne'er-yet-beaten horse of Parthia
We have jaded out o'th'field.

                                          (III.1.30–34)

'That magical word of war' is a sham, and the success comes from calculation and from making sure that the soldiers are 'well-paid'.

By the standards of the play Pompey is a failure. By refusing Menas's offer to make him 'lord of all the world' (II.7.61) he seals his own fate. His murder, casually mentioned in III.5 as a postscript to Lepidus's fall from power, is the only possible outcome of his failing to authorise the killing of the triumvirate.

In refusing Menas, Pompey specifically separates the concept of honour from political success:

In me 'tis villainy;
In thee't had been good service. Thou must know
'Tis not my profit that does lead mine honour;
Mine honour, it.

                                          (II.7.74–77)

But honour doesn't exist in separation from political action. 'Your honour calls you hence' (I.3.97) says Cleopatra, having demolished Antony's wish to see the concept as innate, something which he holds simply because he is Antony:

Good now, play one scene
Of excellent dissembling, and let it look
Like perfect honour.

                                          (I.3.78–80)

When facing Caesar for the first time, Antony's words show that 'honour' is, in practical terms, a synonym for political credibility: 'The honour is sacred which he talks on now,/ Supposing that I lacked it' (II.2.89–90), and his final advice to Cleopatra, 'Of Caesar seek your honour, with your safety' (IV.15.46), stresses this truth and shows up the myth which destroyed Pompey.

This essay's title comes from the moment when Antony is recognising the nature of the terms he uses to define himself. At first reading, his words may seem a simple extension of the images of 'melting' and 'changing substance' which can be found throughout the second half of the play:

Sometimes we see a cloud that's dragonish,
A vapour sometime like a bear or lion,
A towered citadel, a pendent rock,
A forkèd mountain, or blue promontory
With trees upon't that nod unto the world
And mock our eyes with air.
  . . .
That which is now a horse, even with a thought
The rack dislimns, and makes it indistinct
As water is in water.
                    . . . now thy captain is
Even such a body. Here I am Antony,
Yet cannot hold this visible shape, my knave.

(IV.14.2–14)

But the cloud remains a cloud. The shapes which are perceived
are the product of the eye and can vanish 'even with a thought'.
And just as the perceived shapes find their being in the human
memory and imagination, so Antony's 'visible shape', 'thy captain',
is not a quality found in Antony but a reflection of what others
want to see in him. Antony's substance does not melt or change;
to read the passage as if that is what is signified would be to
claim that it is not our eyes which impose the patterns of
dragons, citadels or horses on transient cloud-formations, but
that these shapes are there even if no one looks at them.
Looking creates what is seen, just as the qualities and titles in
Antony and Cleopatra are produced by the political circumstances.

It is in the possibility of realising this that the play is
significantly different from other Shakespearean tragedies. At
one level the tragedy works in the audience's awareness of the
gap between the way in which the protagonists see themselves
and the way we see them. However, in this play we are continually reminded of the impermanence of these descriptions. To
begin with, there is a degree of self-consciousness in the imagery
which undercuts any attempt to read it as a definition. For
example, the principal effect of Enobarbus's description of
Cleopatra (II.2.195–223) is to highlight her humanity rather
than any goddesslike qualities. The dominant mode of description is simile; 'like smiling cupids' (line 207) and 'like the

Nereides' (line 211) stress that the boys are really boys, the gentlewomen women, and that they reminded the Roman visitors of the supernatural world. Simile, simply by using 'like' or 'as', signals that the two parts of the comparison are essentially different from each other. The barge is 'like a burnished throne' (line 196) but it isn't a burnished throne; it's a barge. It is not a mermaid but 'A seeming mermaid' (line 214) who steers. The images are as consciously based in the onlookers as are the shapes seen in the clouds. For Cleopatra, Antony is not a Gorgon or a Mars but: 'Though he be painted one way like a Gorgon,/ The other way's a Mars.' (II.5.116–117). When the more direct mode of metaphor is used, there is still this self-consciousness which will not allow us to imagine that she forgets Antony's humanity in calling him 'The demi-Atlas of this earth' (I.5.23), or that there isn't ironic self-awareness in her claim to have been 'A morsel for a monarch' (I.5.31). The exchange between Enobarbus and Agrippa in III.2 highlights the absurdity of taking metaphor literally. They are mocking Lepidus's attempts to flatter both Caesar and Antony:

> ENOBARBUS   Caesar? Why he's the Jupiter of men.
> AGRIPPA   What's Antony? The god of Jupiter.
> ENOBARBUS   Spake you of Caesar? How! The nonpareil!
> AGRIPPA   O Antony! O thou Arabian bird!
>
> (III.2.9–12)

A few lines further on there is one of the most startling images in the play, and it is worth examining why this is so. Antony is talking about Octavia, her incapacity to form the right public words for the parting from her brother:

> Her tongue will not obey her heart, nor can
> Her heart inform her tongue — the swan's-down feather
> That stands upon the swell at the full of tide,
> And neither way inclines.
>
> (III.2.46–49)

Even if the scansion could be changed to include 'as' in line 47, or if the wording could be altered to make the image a metaphor, the impact would be diminished. Its striking quality lies in the simple juxtaposition of the statement about Octavia and the picture of the most delicate of feathers held static by the exact balance of up and down stream flows. When the syntax signals the similarities, self-consciousness takes over.

This is central to our response to Cleopatra. At Antony's death, 'The crown o'th'earth doth melt' (IV.15.63) derives its power both from the imaginative demands the metaphor makes on our senses and cultural memories, and from the realisation that Cleopatra knows that it is an image. It is for her that Antony has this significance, and the wealth of 'world imagery' she uses of him serves, paradoxically, to stress the deeply personal nature of her vision. This directly reflects the age from which Shakespeare's text springs; this awareness of cultural change is explained by Kiernan Ryan:

> For complex reasons rooted in the levelling, democratising logic of the market economy, the Renaissance engenders an altogether new dimension of human experience and awareness. On the foundations of the nascent Exchange-value system, defined by Marx as 'a system of general social metabolism, of universal social relations, of all-round needs and universal capacities', there begins to rise an egalitarian consciousness of the *virtual* common humanity uniting people across divisions which can now be seen to be socially constructed and arbitrary rather than God-given or natural.[1]

Cleopatra's images of Antony spring from the knowledge that they are her own images; her reassurance of Charmian and Iras is her common humanity:

> No more but e'en a woman, and commanded
> By such poor passion as the maid that milks
> And does the meanest chares.

(IV.15.72–74)

Her embracing of this is in striking contrast to Caesar's perception of the divisions in society. It is shameful to him to point out to Octavia 'But you are come/ A market maid to Rome' (III.6.50–51).

Cleopatra is a queen and yet she has gone beyond seeing the title as a definition. It is from the strength of being 'No more but

---

[1] Kiernan Ryan, *Shakespeare (Harvester New Readings)* (London, 1989), p. 29.

e'en a woman' that her final command can separate herself from her function: 'Show me, my women, like a queen' (V.2.227). Although she is referred to as queen over thirty times, those few occasions when she uses the term herself show an acute awareness of the title as a title rather than a definition. Twice in Act I (I.1.29–30 and I.3.24–25) the tone is elusive, she is goading Antony about their relationship by alluding to her political status: 'As I am Egypt's Queen,/ Thou blushest, Antony,' and 'O, never was there queen/ So mightily betrayed!' It is when addressing Romans, the agents of a Caesar in whose interests it is to believe that political status is natural, that she theatrically implores death to 'come, and take a queen/ Worth many babes and beggars!' (V.2.47–48). Her anger does not diminish the irony.

It is also Cleopatra who points us to an awareness of the self-conscious nature of action. Metaphors derived from the theatre run through the text but it is only for Caesar that play-acting is in opposition to reality. From the beginning, Antony and Cleopatra conduct themselves in full awareness of an audience. This is not the audience in the theatre but the other actors who are on stage with them. Their embrace in public is a theatrical declaration: 'The nobleness of life/ Is to do thus' (I.1.36–37) proclaims Antony. Act I scene 3 reveals an acute awareness on Cleopatra's part that they are both 'acting', that is, they are fitting into clearly defined roles which are entirely social constructs and therefore arbitrary, in order to express themselves. 'Look, prithee, Charmian,/ How this Herculean Roman does become/ The carriage of his chafe' (lines 83–85) exploits the gap between the fumbling human being and the sense of identity which the Romans feel is incapsulated in the god Hercules and the title 'Roman'. Cleopatra is sincere in her farewell but she is also well aware of the way in which she is using the language of a specific culture:

> Upon your sword
> Sit laurel victory, and smooth success
> Be strewed before your feet!

> (I.3.99–101)

Cleopatra's awareness of her own theatricality is embraced. Fun was theatrical fun: 'Then [I] put my tires and mantles on him, whilst/ I wore his sword Philippan' (II.5.22–23). When she attempts to express her love for Antony without using these conventions, the language aspires to a level at which it dissociates itself from terms of social reference:

> Sir, you and I must part, but that's not it.
> Sir, you and I have loved, but there's not it.
> That you know well. Something it is I would —
> O my oblivion is a very Antony,
> And I am all forgotten.

(I.3.87–91)

The fragile dignity of this speech comes from its avoiding all the shorthand implicit in simile and metaphor. The essence of human relationship cannot be expressed in social terminology but still we cannot pretend that social constructs don't inform the way we express ourselves, and so she is obliged to fall back on a list of negatives.

Both Antony and Cleopatra know that theatricality has its capacity to become humiliation. In urging Eros to kill him, Antony has only to mention the possibility of this reversal: 'Wouldst thou be windowed in great Rome and see/ Thy master thus' (IV.14.72–73), and in V.2 Cleopatra draws a vivid picture of mocking theatre (lines 208–221) culminating in 'Some squeaking Cleopatra boy my greatness/ I'th'posture of a whore'. But this does not mean a rejection of all theatricality as demeaning. That judgement is Caesar's. It is he who sees their staged act of political assertion as a disgrace:

> I'th'market-place on a tribunal silvered,
> Cleopatra and himself in chairs of gold
> Were publicly enthroned

(III.6.3–5)

Caesar's mind rejects acting and costume because he finds it necessary to believe in essential immutable character. His breaking up of the party on Pompey's galley is revealing: 'The wild disguise hath almost/ Anticked us all' (II.7.122–123). While Antony and Cleopatra are consciously performing for an audience, Caesar's public face is for a historian, a sober reporter:

> Go with me to my tent, where you shall see
> How hardly I was drawn into this war,

> How calm and gentle I proceeded still
> In all my writings.
>
> (V.1.73–76)

Antony and Cleopatra illuminate each other; their language faces up to their own transience. She is the 'day o'th'world' (IV.8.13), and for him her death is the onset of darkness: 'since the torch is out/ Lie down, and stray no farther' (IV.14.46–47). Cleopatra echoes this with 'Our lamp is spent, it's out' (IV.15.84). Compare the impact of this with the images of light in other plays. When Othello is about to murder Desdemona he sees a simple correspondence between light and life; he contemplates the parallel between extinguishing a candle and extinguishing his wife's life: 'Put out the light, and then put out the light' (*Othello*, V.2.7). 'Out, out, brief candle!' (*Macbeth*, V.5.23) says Macbeth but he does see a more involved relationship between light and life than does Othello. For him 'Life's but a walking shadow' (V.5.24). A shadow requires an object, something on which to cast the shadow and the light itself. Othello does not imagine himself in darkness once Desdemona is dead; Macbeth's nihilism sees life itself as illusory. But for Antony and Cleopatra the other is the light which illuminates their acting; death is when the light goes down and the play ends: 'Finish, good lady,' says Iras, 'the bright day is done,/ And we are for the dark' (V.2.193–194).

We are constantly aware of the contingent nature of all the statements in the play, but there is a marked difference in the degree to which the two main characters accept the lack of fixed definition and certainty. Antony is continually frustrated by his inability to freeze time; Cleopatra is infuriating because she doesn't want the same amusement two days running: 'Last night you did desire it' (I.1.55). The 'did' signals a world of frustration. More harrowing for Antony is the realisation that political status isn't inherent in his simply being Antony; it is humiliating to hear Caesar 'harping on what I am,/ Not what he knew I was' (III.13.142–143), and, as has already been pointed out, his final comfort is in the contemplation of 'my former fortunes' (IV.15.53). On the other hand Cleopatra always accepts the force of context: 'That time — O times!' (II.5.18) could be her motto. 'When' and 'then' constantly preface her remarks, and the effect is to disarm any attempt to see the play as a group of fixed characters moving through a variety of situations. 'When you sued staying,/ Then was the time for words' (I.3.32–33); 'My salad days,/ When I was green in judgement' (I.5.74–75): while the impact here has an ironic edge, the cumulative effect of such remarks is to push us to an awareness of the arbitrary nature of the social contexts from which apparently timeless judgements arise. She recognises the uncompromising unsentimentality of time in her acceptance of how futile it is to dream of Antony and Caesar in single combat. The full weight of the statement is carried by the simple words 'then' and 'now':

> That he and Caesar might
> Determine this great war in single fight!
> Then Antony — but now.
>
> (IV.4.36–38)

In the context of the play the Soothsayer suggests an awful inevitability in the course of events. Both his apparently light-hearted prophecies to Charmian and Iras, and his doom-laden warnings to Antony come true. The question this raises is not so much how he knows, but why these things come about. Antony sees the shapes in the clouds as ominous: 'Thou hast seen these signs;/ They are black vesper's pageants' (IV.14.7–8). In accepting such fatalism Antony is unaware of the questions the play raises for an audience, a pushing back of enquiry beyond the level of personalities to ask why politics, war, brutality and the casual inflicting of suffering — 'Some innocents 'scape not the thunderbolt' (II.5.77) — are taken as necessary and inevitable. Antony's final moments see him embracing abstract terms, 'valour' for example, which seem to have no social context to give them validity. The same Reuter report quoted at the beginning of this essay has a similar response from the deposed Romanian dictator. When asked why people were starving: '"This is a lie," Ceausescu stubbornly told his interrogator. "Think carefully. It is a lie and proves the lack of patriotism currently in the country."' 'Patriotism' has become no more than an empty noise, a prop for a condemned man's sense of his own innate qualities. One of the things which *Antony and Cleopatra* shows us is that the real 'cloud that's dragonish' is the crippling acceptance of the arbitrary and the contingent as if they were inevitable and eternal, a final clinging to empty terms, 'academician', 'the greatest prince o'th'world'.

AFTERTHOUGHTS

1

How appropriate is it to compare Antony and Cleopatra to contemporary East European dictators?

2

What difference does Spencer Ellis highlight between Pompey's and Antony's understanding of 'honour' (page 96)?

3

'Looking creates what is seen' (page 97): how important is this point to *Antony and Cleopatra* as a whole?

4

What difference does Spencer Ellis highlight between Antony's and Cleopatra's attitude to time (pages 102–103)?

John E Cunningham

*John E Cunningham currently divides
his time between writing and travel. He
is the author of numerous critical
studies.*

ESSAY

Antony and Cleopatra:
the world well lost

When, seventy years after Shakespeare, Dryden produced his
version of the story of Antony and Cleopatra, he called it *All for
Love or The World Well Lost*. This title made clear to the
narrow, court audience for whom he wrote what they were to
think of his treatment: this was a story of overriding passion.
The tragic conventions of his day obliged him to confine the
action to a single place, the Temple of Isis, and to the last few
hours in the lives of the chief characters. The effect is of a
concentrated but limited drama. Shakespeare, on the other
hand, could suggest a vast sweep of events embracing the whole
of the known world, notably in the notorious third Act with its
thirteen scenes, to show the widespread upheaval caused by
individual action; while at the very beginning of the play we are
apparently told that it is not about love but infatuation, the
diminution of a once-great man — 'The triple pillar of the world
transformed/ Into a strumpet's fool' (I.1.12–13). The play's theme
seems to be the conflict between Rome, the stern 'world' of
affairs, duties, practicalities — and Egypt, decadent, pleasure-
loving, where queens idly play anachronistic billiards and chat
with their bawdy maids. Rome triumphs in the end, as Rome did
in fact, though there have been critics to argue that that is not

the sense of the play. Perhaps few would go so far as C J Sisson, and say 'To turn death itself into a triumph is an achievement of Christianity and of romantic drama'. Yet the whole presentation of responsibility versus what Philo, in the very first line of the play, calls 'this dotage of our general' strikes us as much too complicated to be containable within some moral maxim on the lines of: Always do your duty and avoid exta-marital affairs.

We have said that Rome triumphed in fact, and with facts we may begin. Cleopatra was not, as Philo calls her in the speech already quoted, a gipsy, nor an 'Egyptian dish' as she is later described, nor 'with Phoebus' amorous pinches black' as she says of herself (I.5.28). She had no Egyptian blood at all but was of Greek — Macedonian — descent. She not only spoke Greek but was the first of her royal line to take the trouble to master Egyptian as well as Ethiopian, Hebrew, Aramaic, Syriac and two sorts of Persian. As to her appearance, coins suggest she wore a Greek hairstyle or possibly a wig, and had an over-prominent nose. Early historians speak of her as having a radiant quality, a very attractive voice, above all a fascinating manner rather than an obvious beauty. The world she repre-sented, and for which she continually schemed, was not that of 'Egypt' but of the wide sphere of Greek influence in the East. Under this alien dynasty, the Egyptians retained an individu-ality which they still have, while the split between East and West survives to this day in the break between the Roman Catholic and Orthodox churches. Cleopatra did indeed fascinate both Julius Caesar, uncle of Octavius, and, as a mature woman, Antony, by both of whom she had children. Octavius Caesar killed his cousin and in due course, his rival and his rival's mistress both having committed suicide, became Augustus, the first Roman emperor.

Shakespeare certainly knew the work of one of the historians mentioned above, Plutarch, of whom there was a popular trans-lation available in his day. He drew on it for the famous description given by Enobarbus (II.2.191 onwards) of the first meeting between the lovers. A few lines later he sums her up, in phrases some of which have become a part of the language:

> Age cannot wither her, nor custom stale
> Her infinite variety. Other women cloy

> The appetites they feed, but she makes hungry
> Where most she satisfies; for vilest things
> Become themselves in her, that the holy priests
> Bless her when she is riggish.

(II.2.240–245)

This is a good point of departure for our own attempt to explore the play: to see if Dryden's interpretation of it will hold; to try to come to some conclusions about what Shakespeare intended us to make of the worlds of Rome and Egypt through their representatives; to ask, as Cleopatra does in her very first line 'if it be love indeed', and whether the world was well lost for it.

It is a good point for two reasons: it is praise by a hostile critic, for Enobarbus, like so many of Antony's friends, regrets and resents her influence upon him; and it tries to make sense of what is, in the end, beyond sense, the irrational power of a fascinating woman, a *femme fatale*. Though this is a common theme of fiction, stretching from Eve to Zola's Nana, even as the infatuated man may be traced from Adam to Nabokov's Humbert Humbert, it is one that is very hard to make convincing without causing the reader to reflect, perhaps smugly, either that such a woman is impossible in 'real' life or that such a man must be a fool. It was especially hard for Shakespeare to present irresistible attraction on the stage of his day, where, as he makes the Queen herself say, with a kind of breathtaking theatrical cheek:

> I shall see
> Some squeaking Cleopatra boy my greatness

(V.2.219–220)

Yet it is not altogether impossible that a lively adolescent boy-actor should have been able to present precisely some of the fascination Enobarbus talks of when he says he has seen her:

> Hop forty paces through the public street;
> And, having lost her breath, she spoke, and panted,
> That she did make defect perfection

(II.2.234–236)

There is, if not a tomboyish, an epicene quality here that can be most attractive, especially when it is set against the gravity of the world of the Roman matron to whom Antony owed his duty as a husband. And again and again we are shown someone who is unpredictable, so that no one quite knows where he is with her. She can flatter a messenger, mock a lover, be all submission to a conqueror, feign a death to bring a man to heel — and die herself when she knows she will otherwise be humiliated, though she had not scrupled to humiliate Antony at the battle of Actium.

The play was written early in the reign of James I, and it is often said of Jacobean tragedy that the crucial test of its characters is how they face their own death. The whole scene of Cleopatra's suicide is magnificent stage — a cynic might say magnificently staged; but at the heart of it there is something that comes very close to us, the audience. This theme is announced at the end of Antony's death:

> No more but e'en a woman, and commanded
> By such poor passion as the maid that milks
> And does the meanest chares

(IV.15.72–74)

and is confirmed in her final lines:

> Peace, peace!
> Dost thou not see my baby at my breast,
> That sucks the nurse asleep?

(V.2.307–309)

These images are of the utmost simplicity, and remind us — her too, perhaps — that Royal Egypt is just as other women are, subject to the same griefs and delights, and far transcend the limitations of the fourteen-year-old boy-actor who might have uttered them.

Having tried to weigh the imponderable and assess something of her fascination, we may turn to her lover and his 'dotage'. We must at once ask what was the conventional view of headlong devotion to a woman — however wonderful — in Shakespeare's day; and the answer is not favourable for Antony. Women were the subordinate sex, as in many parts of the world they still are quite officially, and for a woman to dominate a man was a reversal of the supposed natural order of things, a crime against society: hence the treatment of scolds and shrews; hence the law that if a woman killed her husband it was not just murder but minor treason. It is hard today to make a good production of *The Taming of the Shrew*, which ends with the spirited Katherine — properly, as the audience would then have thought — dominated by her husband Petruchio; but a modern audience's sense of outrage at this may be a little mollified by the feeling that the pair will, in their private lives, continue to strike sparks from each other's lively personalities and enjoy a relationship that is the better for their strengths. This is not the situation with Antony, who is always, in the end, subject to Cleopatra, so that when he thinks she is dead he cannot live without her. Would Shakespeare's contemporaries then have regarded him with the contempt that Caesar expresses — 'He hath given his empire/ Up to a whore' (III.6.66–67)? Here we may remark that, as with Enobarbus and Cleopatra, the most striking tribute paid to Antony is by someone who does not much like him, Caesar himself. Urging Antony to 'leave thy lascivious wassails', he recalls the man who, in the most formidable of campaign conditions:

> . . . didst drink
> The stale of horses, and the gilded puddle
> Which beasts would cough at.
> . . .
>
> On the Alps
> It is reported thou didst eat strange flesh,
> Which some did die to look on. And all this —
> It wounds thine honour that I speak it now —
> Was borne so like a soldier that thy cheek
> So much as lanked not.

(I.4.61–63, 66–71)

This is 'Roman' praise: Caesar approves in him those virtues of austerity and patriotic soldiership which were the old ideals of the Republic. Not everyone in the audience will see them as the only values, nor find them on their own wholly appealing — a point we shall have to consider in looking at Caesar himself.

Our ambivalent feelings about Antony may be compared with those we have for another problematic hero who shared his virtue of courage to a high degree and who was also susceptible to female influence: Macbeth. What makes both these men sympathetic to an audience — though in this, Antony is far more successful — is that both are deeply aware of themselves, of the nature of the deeds they do, of the direction in which they are going, yet which they seem impotent to change. Like Macbeth, Antony lives to find himself deserted, his fair-weather friends gone:

> The hearts
> That spanieled me at heels, to whom I gave
> Their wishes, do discandy, melt their sweets
> On blossoming Caesar; and this pine is barked
> That overtopped them all. Betrayed I am.
> O this false soul of Egypt! This grave charm,
> Whose eye becked forth my wars, and called them home,
> Whose bosom was my crownet, my chief end,
> Like a right gypsy hath at fast and loose
> Beguiled me to the very heart of loss.
>
> (IV.12.20–29)

No one is harder on him than he is himself, no one sees better the truth of his position, the destructive nature of his passion.

Antony, then, may be seen as a man with a Roman capacity to eat strange flesh upon the Alps, but also with a fondness for revelling long o'nights as Julius Caesar said of him in the earlier play: the old lion may be dying, may be Antony yet, but the beds in the East are soft. He is pulled between two worlds and so destroyed: the business of life is taken over, as it must be, by those who have no such weaknesses in their nature. To complete our assessment we need to look a little more into Rome's chief representative, on whom this duty devolves.

Caesar is seen at his best, and perhaps his worst, in Act III scene 6, where he is receiving the latest news of Antony's scandalous behaviour and trying to comfort the deeply wronged Octavia, who had hoped to be the instrument of their reconciliation. His tone is icy in the extreme, puritanical in its disgust, insensitive to his sister's feelings:

> at the feet sat
> Caesari-n, whom they call my father's son,
> And all the unlawful issue that their lust
> Since then had made between them.
>
> (III.6.5–8)

Quick to defend by suggestion rather than fact the purity of his adoptive 'father', who appears to have had the sexual morals of a goat (and he later killed Caesarion just in case) he is less than tactless in comforting Octavia; when she says that she asked Antony's pardon for wishing to return to Rome, her brother chimes in:

> Which soon he granted,
> Being an obstruct 'tween his lust and him.

(III.6.60–61)

But he does what he can for her, in his stern, dutiful way. There is the same sense of a flicker of generosity trying to break through the bonds of an austere nature in his attitude to the war with Antony. He can regret that old comrades should come to this pass:

> But yet let me lament
> With tears as sovereign as the blood of hearts,
> That thou, my brother, my competitor
> In top of all design, my mate in empire,
> Friend and companion in the front of war . . .

(V.1.40–44)

yet the same man can coolly order those who had deserted to him, that is those who had put their final trust in his mercy, should be placed in the front rank of the attack: good policy, because it will dishearten their attackers to be faced with their former friends; heartless, because the men who have turned to support him will be the first to be killed. And in the scene we have just quoted, he plots quite cold-bloodedly to take Cleopatra alive because her presence as a captive would be 'eternal in our triumph'. The use of 'our' here sounds very much as if he is already using the royal plural and sees himself as emperor.

Finally we may note that if there is truth in wine, as the proverb has it, the three triumvirs are put to the vinous test on Pompey's galley, where they meet in supposed good fellowship. Antony remains as always a little larger than life, enjoying the revels, heedless of the morning after:

> Come, let's all take hands
> Till that the conquering wine hath steeped our sense

In soft and delicate Lethe.

(II.7.104–106)

Lepidus quickly becomes drunk and foolish in his cups and has to be carried out — so much for the ruler of Africa. But Caesar remains fastidiously uncomfortable, a priggish spectre at the feast. If he represents the world that Dryden said was well lost, it is certainly a world a bit too good for most of us. And when the worlds of Rome and Egypt meet — when Caesar finally enters the monument to ask, with feigned innocence, which of them is the Queen — he lies with the greatest smoothness, promising safety to her and to her children, just as she lies to him about the record of her riches. But when he has left, vowing her every sort of security, we find she is the better judge of character — 'he words me, girls,' she cries, knowing he means nothing of what he has said, determined on suicide 'after the high Roman fashion'. Caesar does not well understand women, a small part of his world; Cleopatra rarely misjudges men, so important in hers. So she passes through the black humour of the understated scene with the Clown to the solemnities of the robing and to the oddly gentle end, with its suggestion of rejoining her lover. It is left to Rome to say the last official word, as Rome always does, and as Caesar had already done at the end of *Julius Caesar* to mark himself as the rising star. Then too he had to pay some sort of tribute to an enemy, to Brutus. Antony, who had himself pursued Brutus with implacable hatred to his death, speaks first, and pays the dead man the most magnanimous of personal compliments: 'This was a man'. Young Octavius Caesar more temperately says 'According to his virtue let us use him'. Virtue, that very Roman concept of duty, courage physical and mental, admirable yet cold, is to be given its exact reward, no more. Since then, this young man has perhaps learned a little more humanity, and can concede:

> . . . their story is
> No less in pity than his glory . . .

(V.2.359–360)

and he gives orders for the two to be buried together — we seem to have come a long way ourselves from the dotage and the strumpet's fool — but his mind is already on the return to the capital of that world of which he was to become the not undistinguished ruler. While we must all agree that a world ruled by Antony and Cleopatra would soon be in chaos, we might wish for more humanity in our leaders than Augustus Caesar seems to offer. Shakespeare seems to have been often drawn to explore the paradoxes that arise when a man's personality is at odds with his station in life — we can see this in Richard II, perhaps in Hamlet, surely in Antony, right through to the very last play, *The Tempest*, in which Prospero admits to having been unsuited by personal disposition to his rank and duty as Duke of Milan.

But Shakespeare, unlike many of his critics, does not seem to judge, only to delineate. When Dryden tackled this story, he prefaced it by a long argument in the course of which he said, 'for the crimes of love, which they both committed, were not occasioned by any necessity, or fatal ignorance, but were wholly voluntary; since our passions are, or ought to be, in our power'. Shakespeare was fascinated by the world as it is, not as it 'ought to be'. And on the complicated subject of 'the crimes of love', which we set out to explore, we shall see that he knew better than Dryden.

It used to be a commentators' whim to pursue the theme of some dark charmer from Shakespeare's private life, through all the brunettes who appear — or don't — in his plays; from Cleopatra herself to the unseen Rosaline with whom Romeo is at first besotted, all linked with the famous Dark Lady of the Sonnets. That Lady has been identified beyond all doubt — differently — by many scholars, has even been held to be a Dark Gentleman: but in one Sonnet not especially addressed to anyone, Shakespeare says everything there is to say about inordinate sexual attraction. This is No. 129: 'Th'expense of Spirit in a waste of shame'. Relentlessly he catalogues the madness of desire, the inevitable disappointment when it is achieved, the fever of anticipation, the post-coital tristesse . . . and then ends with a simple, inescapable couplet:

> All this the world well knows, yet none know well
> To shun the heaven that leads men to this hell.

Men, in other words, have always been able to understand the nature of their own folly — and have gone on committing it. Vast changes in attitudes towards sexual relationships — I alone have lived through three, caused by the War, the Pill and AIDS, the last one still being worked out — do not diminish the truth of this. This is how we are.

We began this exploration with a few facts, and to a fact of human nature we have returned: let us end with a speculation.

Pascal, who is said so to have abhorred women that he would not let his mother kiss him, wrote in his *Pensées*, 'If Cleopatra's nose had been shorter, the whole face of the earth would have been changed.' He may have been wrong about the nose, but in essence he is right: if she had not had some fascination that could not be resisted, Antony would presumably have remained faithful to his wife and triumviral duty, Caesar would not have become the first emperor of the then known world, there would be no play for us to read and if there were I should not be writing these lines about it in a month called August. As it was, Antony did indeed lose his world, but whether well or ill, whether for love or folly, Shakespeare does not tell us: he leaves such certainties for lesser men like Dryden.

AFTERTHOUGHTS

1

How does Cunningham's interpretation of Caesar's question as to which woman is Cleopatra (page 112) differ from Reynolds's (page 79)? Which interpretation do you favour?

2

Do you agree that 'Cleopatra rarely misjudges men' (page 112)?

3

Do you agree that Shakespeare 'does not seem to judge, only to deliniate' his characters (page 113)?

4

Explain the relevance to Cunningham's argument of the sonnet quoted near the end of this essay (page 113).

INTRODUCTION

First, a word of warning. Good essays are the product of a creative engagement with literature. So never try to restrict your studies to what you think will be 'useful in the exam'. Ironically, you will restrict your grade potential if you do.

This doesn't mean, of course, that you should ignore the basic skills of essay writing. When you read critics, make a conscious effort to notice *how* they communicate their ideas. The guidelines that follow offer advice of a more explicit kind. But they are no substitute for practical experience. It is never easy to express ideas with clarity and precision. But the more often you tackle the problems involved and experiment to find your own voice, the more fluent you will become. So practise writing essays as often as possible.

HOW TO PLAN AN ESSAY

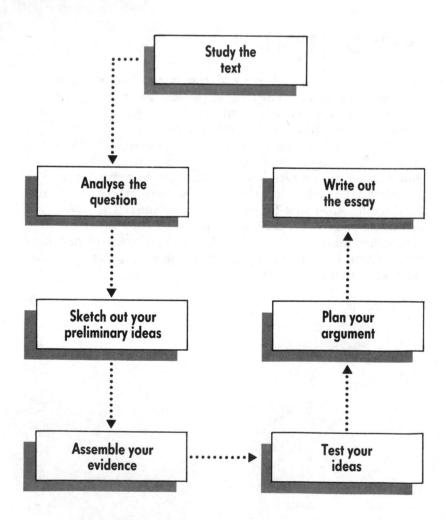

Study the text

The first step in writing a good essay is to get to know the set text well. Never write about a text until you are fully familiar with it. Even a discussion of the opening chapter of a novel, for example, should be informed by an understanding of the book as a whole. Literary texts, however, are by their very nature complex and on a first reading you are bound to miss many significant features. Re-read the book with care, if possible more than once. Look up any unfamiliar words in a good dictionary and if the text you are studying was written more than a few decades ago, consult the *Oxford English Dictionary* to find out whether the meanings of any terms have shifted in the intervening period.

Good books are difficult to put down when you first read them. But a more leisurely second or third reading gives you the opportunity to make notes on those features you find significant. An index of characters and events is often useful, particularly when studying novels with a complex plot or time scheme. The main aim, however, should be to record your *responses* to the text. By all means note, for example, striking images. But be sure to add *why* you think them striking. Similarly, record any thoughts you may have on interesting comparisons with other texts, puzzling points of characterisation, even what you take to be aesthetic blemishes. The important thing is to annotate fully and adventurously. The most seemingly idiosyncratic comment may later lead to a crucial area of discussion which you would otherwise have overlooked. It helps to have a working copy of the text in which to mark up key passages and jot down marginal comments (although obviously these practices are taboo when working with library, borrowed or valuable copies!). But keep a fuller set of notes as well and organise these under appropriate headings.

Literature does not exist in an aesthetic vacuum, however, and you should try to find out as much as possible about the context of its production and reception. It is particularly important to read other works by the same author and writings by contemporaries. At this early stage, you may want to restrict your secondary reading to those standard reference works, such as biographies, which are widely available in public libraries. In the long run, however, it pays to read as wide a range of critical studies as possible.

Some students, and tutors, worry that such studies may stifle the development of any truly personal response. But this won't happen if you are alert to the danger and read critically. After all, you wouldn't passively accept what a stranger told you in conversation. The fact that a critic's views are in print does not necessarily make them any more authoritative (as a glance at the review pages of the *TLS* and *London Review of Books* will reveal). So question the views you find: 'Does this critic's interpretation agree with mine and where do we part company?' 'Can it be right to try and restrict this text's meanings to those found by its author or first audience?' 'Doesn't this passage treat a theatrical text as though it were a novel?' Often it is views which you reject which prove most valuable since they challenge you to articulate your own position with greater clarity. Be sure to keep careful notes on what the critic wrote, and your *reactions* to what the critic wrote.

Analyse the question

You cannot begin to answer a question until you understand what task it is you have been asked to perform. Re-cast the question in your own words and reconstruct the line of reasoning which lies behind it. Where there is a choice of topics, try to choose the one for which you are best prepared. It would, for example, be unwise to tackle 'How far do you agree that in *Paradise Lost* Milton transformed the epic models he inherited from ancient Greece and Rome?' without a working knowledge of Homer and Virgil (or *Paradise Lost* for that matter!). If you do not already know the works of these authors, the question should spur you on to read more widely — or discourage you from attempting it at all. The scope of an essay, however, is not always so obvious and you must remain alert to the implied demands of each question. How could you possibly 'Consider the view that *Wuthering Heights* transcends the conventions of the Gothic novel' without reference to at least some of those works which, the question suggests, have *not* transcended Gothic conventions?

When you have decided on a topic, analyse the terms of the question itself. Sometimes these self-evidently require careful definition: *tragedy* and *irony*, for example, are notoriously difficult concepts to pin down and you will probably need to consult a good dictionary of literary terms. Don't ignore, however, those seemingly innocuous phrases which often smuggle in significant assumptions. 'Does Macbeth lack the nobility of the true tragic hero?' obviously invites you to discuss nobility and the nature of the tragic hero. But what of 'lack' and 'true' — do they suggest that the play would be improved had Shakespeare depicted Macbeth in a different manner? or that tragedy is superior to other forms of drama? Remember that you are not expected meekly to agree with the assumptions implicit in the question. Some questions are deliberately provocative in order to stimulate an engaged response. Don't be afraid to take up the challenge.

Sketch out your preliminary ideas

'Which comes first, the evidence or the answer?' is one of those chicken and egg questions. How can you form a view without inspecting the evidence? But how can you know which evidence is relevant without some idea of what it is you are looking for? In practice the mind reviews evidence and formulates preliminary theories or hypotheses at one and the same time, although for the sake of clarity we have separated out the processes. Remember that these early ideas are only there to get you started. You *expect* to modify them in the light of the evidence you uncover. Your initial hypothesis may be an instinctive 'gut-reaction'. Or you may find that you prefer to 'sleep on the problem', allowing ideas to gell over a period of time. Don't worry in either case. The mind is quite capable of processing a vast amount of accumulated evidence, the product of previous reading and thought, and reaching sophisticated intuitive judgements. Eventually, however, you are going to have to think carefully through any ideas you arrive at by such intuitive processes. Are they logical? Do they take account of all the relevant factors? Do they fully answer the question set? Are there any obvious reasons to qualify or abandon them?

Assemble your evidence

Now is the time to return to the text and re-read it with the question and your working hypothesis firmly in mind. Many of the notes you have already made are likely to be useful, but assess the precise relevance of this material and make notes on any new evidence you discover. The important thing is to cast your net widely and take into account points which tend to undermine your case as well as those that support it. As always, ensure that your notes are full, accurate, and reflect your own critical judgements.

You may well need to go outside the text if you are to do full justice to the question. If you think that the 'Oedipus complex' may be relevant to an answer on *Hamlet* then read Freud and a balanced selection of those critics who have discussed the appropriateness of applying psychoanalytical theories to the interpretation of literature. Their views can most easily be tracked down by consulting the annotated bibliographies held by most major libraries (and don't be afraid to ask a librarian for help in finding and using these). Remember that you go to works of criticism not only to obtain information but to stimulate you into clarifying your own position. And that since life is short and many critical studies are long, judicious use of a book's index and/or contents list is not to be scorned. You can save yourself a great deal of future labour if you carefully record full bibliographic details at this stage.

Once you have collected the evidence, organise it coherently. Sort the detailed points into related groups and identify the quotations which support these. You must also assess the relative importance of each point, for in an essay of limited length it is essential to establish a firm set of priorities, exploring some ideas in depth while discarding or subordinating others.

Test your ideas

As we stressed earlier, a hypothesis is only a proposal, and one that you fully expect to modify. Review it with the evidence before you. Do you really still believe in it? It would be surprising if you did not want to modify it in some way. If you cannot see any problems, others may. Try discussing your ideas with friends and relatives. Raise them in class discussions. Your tutor is certain to welcome your initiative. The critical process is essentially collaborative and there is absolutely no reason why you should not listen to and benefit from the views of others. Similarly, you should feel free to test your ideas against the theories put forward in academic journals and books. But do not just borrow what you find. Critically analyse the views on offer and, where appropriate, integrate them into your own pattern of thought. You must, of course, give full acknowledgement to the sources of such views.

Do not despair if you find you have to abandon or modify significantly your initial position. The fact that you are prepared to do so is a mark of intellectual integrity. Dogmatism is never an academic virtue and many of the best essays explore the *process* of scholarly enquiry rather than simply record its results.

Plan your argument

Once you have more or less decided on your attitude to the question (for an answer is never really 'finalised') you have to present your case in the most persuasive manner. In order to do this you must avoid meandering from point to point and instead produce an organised argument — a structured flow of ideas and supporting evidence, leading logically to a conclusion which fully answers the question. Never begin to write until you have produced an outline of your argument.

You may find it easiest to begin by sketching out its main stages as a flow chart or some other form of visual presentation. But eventually you should produce a list of paragraph topics. The paragraph is the conventional written demarcation for a unit of thought and you can outline an argument quite simply by briefly summarising the substance of each paragraph and then checking that these points (you may remember your English teacher referring to them as topic sentences) really do follow a coherent order. Later you will be able to elaborate on each topic, illustrating and qualifying it as you go along. But you will find this far easier to do if you possess from the outset a clear map of where you are heading.

All questions require some form of an argument. Even so-called 'descriptive' questions *imply* the need for an argument. An adequate answer to the request to 'Outline the role of Iago in *Othello*' would do far more than simply list his appearances on stage. It would at the very least attempt to provide some *explanation* for his actions — is he, for example, a representative stage 'Machiavel'? an example of pure evil, 'motiveless malignity'? or a realistic study of a tormented personality reacting to identifiable social and psychological pressures?

Your conclusion ought to address the terms of the question. It may seem obvious, but 'how far do you agree', 'evaluate', 'consider', 'discuss', etc, are *not* interchangeable formulas and your conclusion must take account of the precise wording of the question. If asked 'How far do you agree?', the concluding paragraph of your essay really should state whether you are in complete agreement, total disagreement, or, more likely, partial agreement. Each preceding paragraph should have a clear justification for its existence and help to clarify the reasoning which underlies your conclusion. If you find that a paragraph serves no good purpose (perhaps merely summarising the plot), do not hesitate to discard it.

The arrangement of the paragraphs, the overall strategy of the argument, can vary. One possible pattern is dialectical: present the arguments in favour of one point of view (**thesis**); then turn to counter-arguments or to a rival interpretation (**antithesis**); finally evaluate the competing claims and arrive at your own conclusion (**synthesis**). You may, on the other hand, feel so convinced of the merits of one particular case that you wish to devote your entire essay to arguing that viewpoint persuasively (although it is always desirable to indicate, however briefly, that you are aware of alternative, if flawed, positions). As the essays contained in this volume demonstrate, there are many other possible strategies. Try to adopt the one which will most comfortably accommodate the demands of the question and allow you to express your thoughts with the greatest possible clarity.

Be careful, however, not to apply abstract formulas in a mechanical manner. It is true that you should be careful to define your terms. It is *not* true that every essay should begin with 'The dictionary defines x as . . .'. In fact, definitions are often best left until an appropriate moment for their introduction arrives. Similarly every essay should have a beginning, middle and end. But it does not follow that in your opening paragraph you should announce an intention to write an essay, or that in your concluding paragraph you need to signal an imminent desire to put down your pen. The old adages are often useful reminders of what constitutes good practice, but they must be interpreted intelligently.

Write out the essay

Once you have developed a coherent argument you should aim to communicate it in the most effective manner possible. Make certain you clearly identify yourself, and the question you are answering. Ideally, type your answer, or at least ensure your handwriting is legible and that you leave sufficient space for your tutor's comments. Careless presentation merely distracts from the force of your argument. Errors of grammar, syntax and spelling are far more serious. At best they are an irritating blemish, particularly in the work of a student who should be sensitive to the nuances of language. At worst, they seriously confuse the sense of your argument. If you are aware that you have stylistic problems of this kind, ask your tutor for advice at the earliest opportunity. Everyone, however, is liable to commit the occasional howler. The only remedy is to give yourself plenty of time in which to proof-read your manuscript (often reading it aloud is helpful) before submitting it.

Language, however, is not only an instrument of communication; it is also an instrument of thought. If you want to think clearly and precisely you should strive for a clear, precise prose style. Keep your sentences short and direct. Use modern, straightforward English wherever possible. Avoid repetition, clichés and wordiness. Beware of generalisations, simplifications, and overstatements. Orwell analysed the relationship between stylistic vice and muddled thought in his essay 'Politics and the English Language' (1946) — it remains essential reading (and is still readily available in volume 4 of the Penguin *Collected Essays, Journalism and Letters*). Generalisations, for example, are always dangerous. They are rarely true and tend to suppress the individuality of the texts in question. A remark such as 'Keats always employs sensuous language in his poetry' is not only fatuous (what, after all, does it mean? is *every* word he wrote equally 'sensuous'?) but tends to obscure interesting distinctions which could otherwise be made between, say, the descriptions in the 'Ode on a Grecian Urn' and those in 'To Autumn'.

The intelligent use of quotations can help you make your points with greater clarity. Don't sprinkle them throughout your essay without good reason. There is no need, for example, to use them to support uncontentious statements of fact. 'Macbeth murdered Duncan' does not require textual evidence (unless you wish to dispute Thurber's brilliant parody, 'The Macbeth Murder Mystery', which reveals Lady Macbeth's father as the culprit!). Quotations should be included, however, when they are necessary to support your case. The proposition that Macbeth's imaginative powers wither after he has killed his king would certainly require extensive quotation: you would almost certainly want to analyse key passages from both before and after the murder (perhaps his first and last soliloquies?). The key word here is 'analyse'. Quotations cannot make your points on their own. It is up to you to demonstrate their relevance and clearly explain to your readers *why* you want them to focus on the passage you have selected.

Most of the academic conventions which govern the presentation of essays are set out briefly in the style sheet below. The question of gender, however, requires fuller discussion. More than half the population of the world is female. Yet many writers still refer to an undifferentiated *man*kind. Or write of the author and *his* public. We do not think that this convention has much to recommend it. At the very least, it runs the risk of introducing unintended sexist attitudes. And at times leads to such patent absurdities as 'Cleopatra's final speech asserts *man*'s true nobility'. With a little thought, you can normally find ways of expressing yourself which do not suggest that the typical author, critic or reader is male. Often you can simply use plural forms, which is probably a more elegant solution than relying on such awkward formulations as 's/he' or 'he and she'. You should also try to avoid distinguishing between male and female authors on the basis of forenames. Why *Jane* Austen and not *George* Byron? Refer to all authors by their last names unless there is some good reason not to. Where there may otherwise be confusion, say between T S and George Eliot, give the name in full when if first occurs and thereafter use the last name only.

Finally, keep your audience firmly in mind. Tutors and examiners are interested in understanding your conclusions and the processes by which you arrived at them. They are not interested in reading a potted version of a book they already know. **So don't pad out your work with plot summary.**

Hints for examinations

In an examination you should go through exactly the same processes as you would for the preparation of a term essay. The only difference lies in the fact that some of the stages will have had to take place before you enter the examination room. This should not bother you unduly. Examiners are bound to avoid the merely eccentric when they come to formulate papers and if you have read widely and thought deeply about the central issues raised by your set texts you can be confident you will have sufficient material to answer the majority of questions sensibly.

The fact that examinations impose strict time limits makes it *more* rather than less, important that you plan carefully. There really is no point in floundering into an answer without any idea of where you are going, particularly when there will not be time to recover from the initial error.

Before you begin to answer any question at all, study the entire paper with care. Check that you understand the rubric and know how many questions you have to answer and whether any are compulsory. It may be comforting to spot a title you feel confident of answering well, but don't rush to tackle it: read *all* the questions before deciding which *combination* will allow you to display your abilities to the fullest advantage. Once you have made your choice, analyse each question, sketch out your ideas, assemble the evidence, review your initial hypothesis, plan your argument, *before* trying to write out an answer. And make notes at each stage: not only will these help you arrive at a sensible conclusion, but examiners are impressed by evidence of careful thought.

Plan your time as well as your answers. If you have practised writing timed essays as part of your revision, you should not find this too difficult. There can be a temptation to allocate extra time to the questions you know you can answer well; but this is always a short-sighted policy. You will find yourself left to face a question which would in any event have given you difficulty without even the time to give it serious thought. It is, moreover, easier to gain marks at the lower end of the scale than at the upper, and you will never compensate for one poor answer by further polishing two satisfactory answers. Try to leave some time at the end of the examination to re-read your answers and correct any obvious errors. If the worst comes to the worst and you run short of time, don't just keep writing until you are forced to break off in mid-paragraph. It is far better to provide for the examiner a set of notes which indicate the overall direction of your argument.

Good luck — but if you prepare for the examination conscientiously and tackle the paper in a methodical manner, you won't need it!

hands which were folded in her lap. Her face betrayed no emotion.' Why the second sentence? The report is searching for moments of humanity and dignity which help us to come to terms with death.

> The miserable change now at my end
> Lament nor sorrow at, but please your thoughts
> In feeding them with those my former fortunes,
> Wherein I lived; the greatest prince o'th'world,
> The noblest
>
> (IV.15.51–55)

Line references are normally given directly after the quotation, in brackets.

This is not an exact parallel though many of the same comments do still apply. However, an audience does not necessarily respond in the same way as the reader of a newspaper. In particular, Antony's clinging to his titles as a source of comfort to himself and Cleopatra is something we are more prepared to allow him than we are to find 'academician' a valid label for the Ceausescus. What grounds are there for seeing Antony as 'the greatest prince o'th'world', and what are the social forces which make him so eminent?

The political world of *Antony and Cleopatra* is a violent one. While the text allows us to see conflict in terms of character (and generations of examiners have cheerfully reduced the play to high-grade soap opera through questions implying that it is merely a series of personality clashes), we are always aware that conflicts have a price. When Caesar addresses Pompey the acknowledged alternative to a truce is wholesale killing:

long verse quotation, indented and introduced by a colon. Quotation marks are not needed.

book/play title given in italics. In a handwritten or typed manuscript this would appear as underlining: Antony and Cleopatra.

> ... let us know
> If 'twill tie up thy discontented sword
> And carry back to Sicily much tall youth
> That else must perish here.
>
> (II.6.5–8)

Death is the currency of political negotiations. Caesar's offer to Cleopatra after Actium is straightforward — safety: 'so she/ From Egypt drive her all-disgracèd friend/ Or take his life there' (III.12.21–23). The card he plays to prevent Cleopatra from committing suicide is to threaten her children:

> ... you shall bereave yourself
> Of my good purposes, and put your children

Three dots (ellipsis) indicate where words or phrases have been cut from a quotation or when (as here) a quotation begins mid-sentence.

Short verse quotation incorporated into the text of the essay within quotation marks. Line endings are indicated by a slash (/).

We have divided the following information into two sections. Part A describes those rules which it is essential to master no matter what kind of essay you are writing (including examination answers). Part B sets out some of the more detailed conventions which govern the documentation of essays.

PART A: LAYOUT

Titles of texts

Titles of published books, plays (of any length), long poems, pamphlets and periodicals (including newspapers and magazines), works of classical literature, and films should be underlined: e.g. David Copperfield (novel), Twelfth Night (play), Paradise Lost (long poem), Critical Quarterly (periodical), Horace's Ars Poetica (Classical work), Apocalypse Now (film).

Notice how important it is to distinguish between titles and other names. Hamlet is the play; Hamlet the prince. Wuthering Heights is the novel; Wuthering Heights the house. Underlining is the equivalent in handwritten or typed manuscripts of printed italics. So what normally appears in this volume as *Othello* would be written as Othello in your essay.

Titles of articles, essays, short stories, short poems, songs, chapters of books, speeches, and newspaper articles are enclosed in quotation marks; e.g. 'The Flea' (short poem), 'The Prussian Officer' (short story), 'Middleton's Chess Strategies' (article), 'Thatcher Defects!' (newspaper headline).

Exceptions: Underlining titles or placing them within quotation marks does not apply to sacred writings (e.g. Bible, Koran, Old Testament, Gospels) or parts of a book (e.g. Preface, Introduction, Appendix).

It is generally incorrect to place quotation marks around a title of a published book which you have underlined. The exception is 'titles within titles', e.g. 'Vanity Fair': A Critical Study (title of a book about *Vanity Fair*).

Quotations

Short verse quotations of a single line or part of a line should be incorporated within quotation marks as part of the running text of your essay. Quotations of two or three lines of verse are treated in the same way, with line endings indicated by a slash(/). For example:

1 In <u>Julius Caesar</u>, Antony says of Brutus, 'This was the noblest Roman of them all'.
2 The opening of Antony's famous funeral oration, 'Friends, Romans, Countrymen, lend me your ears;/ I come to bury Caesar not to praise him', is a carefully controlled piece of rhetoric.

Longer verse quotations of more than three lines should be indented from the main body of the text and introduced in most cases with a colon. Do not enclose indented quotations within quotation marks. For example:

It is worth pausing to consider the reasons Brutus gives to justify his decision to assassinate Caesar:

> It must be by his death; and for my part,
> I know no personal cause to spurn at him,
> But for the general. He would be crowned.
> How might that change his nature, there's the question.

At first glance his rationale may appear logical . . .

Prose quotations of less than three lines should be incorporated in the text of the essay, within quotation marks. Longer prose quotations should be indented and the quotation marks omitted. For example:

1 Before his downfall, Caesar rules with an iron hand. His political opponents, the Tribunes Marullus and Flavius, are 'put to silence' for the trivial offence of 'pulling scarfs off Caesar's image'.
2 It is interesting to note the rhetorical structure of Brutus's Forum speech:

> Romans, countrymen, and lovers, hear me for my cause, and be silent that you may hear. Believe me for my honour, and have respect to mine honour that you may believe. Censure me in your wisdom, and awake your senses, that you may the better judge.

Tenses: When you are relating the events that occur within a work of fiction or describing the author's technique, it is the convention to use the present tense. Even though Orwell published *Animal Farm* in 1945, the book *describes* the animals' seizure of Manor Farm. Similarly, Macbeth always *murders* Duncan, despite the passage of time.

PART B: DOCUMENTATION

When quoting from verse of more than twenty lines, provide line references: e.g. In 'Upon Appleton House' Marvell's mower moves 'With whistling scythe and elbow strong' (1.393).

Quotations from plays should be identified by act, scene and line references: e.g. Prospero, in Shakespeare's The Tempest, refers to Caliban as 'A devil, a born devil' (IV.1.188). (i.e. Act 4. Scene 1. Line 188).

Quotations from prose works should provide a chapter reference and, where appropriate, a page reference.

Bibliographies should list full details of all sources consulted. The way in which they are presented varies, but one standard format is as follows:

1 Books and articles are listed in alphabetical order by the author's last name. Initials are placed after the surname.
2 If you are referring to a chapter or article within a larger work, you list it by reference to the author of the article or chapter, not the editor (although the editor is also named in the reference).
3 Give (in parentheses) the place and date of publication, e.g. (London, 1962). These details can be found within the book itself. Here are some examples:

> Brockbank, J.P., 'Shakespeare's Histories, English and Roman', in Ricks, C. (ed.) English Drama to 1710 (Sphere History of Literature in the English Language) (London, 1971).
> Gurr, A., 'Richard III and the Democratic Process', Essays in Criticism 24 (1974), pp. 39–47.
> Spivack, B., Shakespeare and the Allegory of Evil (New York, 1958).

Footnotes: In general, try to avoid using footnotes and build your references into the body of the essay wherever possible. When you do use them give the full bibliographic reference to a work in the first instance and then use a short title: e.g. See K. Smidt, <u>Unconformities in Shakespeare's History Plays</u> (London, 1982), pp. 43–47 becomes Smidt (pp. 43–47) thereafter. Do not use terms such as 'ibid.' or 'op. cit.' unless you are absolutely sure of their meaning.

There is a principle behind all this seeming pedantry. The reader ought to be able to find and check your references and quotations as quickly and easily as possible. Give additional information, such as canto or volume number whenever you think it will assist your reader.

SUGGESTIONS FOR FURTHER READING

Cantor, Paul A, *Shakespeare's Rome: Republic and Empire* (Cambridge, 1976)

Dollimore, Jonathan, *Radical Tragedy* (Hemel Hempstead, 1989)

Leggatt, Alexander, *Shakespeare's Political Drama: The History Plays and the Roman Plays* (London, 1989)

Miola, Robert S, *Shakespeare's Rome* (Cambridge, 1983)

Muir, Kenneth, *Antony and Cleopatra: A Critical Study* (Harmondsworth, 1988)

Scott, Michael, *Antony and Cleopatra: Text and Performance* (Basingstoke, 1983)

Simmons, J L, *Shakespeare's Pagan World: The Roman Tragedies* (Virginia, 1988)

Snyder, Susan, 'Patterns of Motion in *Antony and Cleopatra*', in *Shakespeare Survey*, 33 (1980)

Longman Group Limited
*Longman House, Burnt Mill, Harlow, Essex CM20 2JE, England
and Associated Companies throughout the world.*

First published 1990
Seventh impression 1994
ISBN 0 582 06051 6

Set in 10/12 pt Century Schoolbook, Linotron 202
Produced through Longman Malaysia, GPS

Acknowledgement
The editors would like to thank Zachary Leader for his assist-
ance with the style sheet.

The publisher's policy is to use paper manufactured from
sustainable forests.